THE HOUSEPLANT GUIDE

How to Easily Select & Maintain Indoor
Plants

Publisher: Hortlife Publishing
ISBN: 979-8-9918764-0-7

Printed in the United States of America.

THE HOUSEPLANT GUIDE

LEE MILLER

As a seasoned landscape designer, consultant, garden coach, blogger, and lifelong gardener, I have immersed myself in the art of cultivating thriving ecosystems both inside and outside. While not working outdoors, you will find me enjoying and nurturing my collection of houseplants, each unique for its foliage and blooms. I authored this book so that I could share a compilation of my extensive experience, offering insights, tips, and tricks gathered throughout my journey. Within these pages, you will discover the joy and health benefits that houseplants can bring, along with the wisdom I have gained from tending to my diverse collection. Join me on this green adventure, as we cultivate an indoor oasis together.

CONTENTS

Introduction

Welcome to the world of indoor gardening! Whether you have a green thumb or brown, houseplants are a wonderful way of bringing nature into your home, while improving overall air quality and health, and they are simple to grow, providing you have the proper knowledge. Not only do houseplants look beautiful, but they also serve an important purpose in purifying the air through the absorption of pollutants and release of oxygen. There are numerous types of houseplants to choose from, each with their own characteristics and benefits, and studies have shown that simply being in their presence can help to reduce stress and improve overall mood. When it comes to maintaining the health and vigor of your houseplants, it is important to know the specific needs of each plant. Most houseplants prefer bright, indirect light, but some can tolerate low light, while watering needs vary depending on the plant, but once you know what is best for the plant, growing it is easy!

Understanding Lighting & Watering: Different types of houseplants require individual light needs based on their species and household light varies in intensity depending on the season. A plant requiring high light refers to one placed within two to three feet from a southern, western, or south-western exposure. Medium, bright, or indirect lighting refers to an exposure that receives steady light throughout most of the day when placed within two to three feet of an eastern facing window or five feet from a southern or western exposure. Low, or filtered lighting generally refers to a northern or eastern exposure, perhaps near a window, in a bathroom or beneath a skylight, but never in

direct sun. Bright diffused lighting refers to a sunny window with screening or shades, which reduces intensity and causes the light to scatter more evenly.

Watering: Generally, tropical like houseplants tend to prefer higher levels of humidity and moisture, while desert like cacti and succulents are more drought tolerant. When watering your plants use room temperature water, water early in the day and water generously and less often. Allow the top one or two inches of the soil to dry out slightly before watering again. A common query I receive is, "I water my houseplant every day and it is still wilting. What am I doing wrong?" I recommend feeling the soil just below the surface layer. If it is dry, watering deeper and less often is the answer. It is best to keep a saucer under your plant, water a little at a time, and allow the water to seep through the soil. Empty any excess water from the saucer fifteen to thirty minutes after watering. Since the most common way of destroying houseplants is from over-watering, rather than under-watering, monitor your new plants wisely.

Bottom Watering: Some soft-leaved plants such as African Violet, Begonias and Cyclamens do not like water on their leaves and should be watered from below. Immerse the pot in a bowl or fill the plant's saucer with tepid water and allow it to sit for fifteen minutes allowing the plant to absorb any needed moisture. For these plants, I find planting in a self-watering container to be ideal.

Moisture Loving Houseplants: Some moisture loving houseplants such as Marantha (Prayer Plant), Calathea, Philodendron, Chinese Evergreen and Ferns prefer their soil to be kept consistently moist, but not wet. Giving these plants a good watering every other week using filtered or distilled water, with a small drink in between works well.

I have found using these methods has ensured me with plants that thrive for many years. It is more productive to water deeper and less often, while keeping a schedule of once a week or every other week, depending on the plant's needs. With our busy lifestyles, if you think you will forget to water, put a note on your calendar to remind you. I know I do! While using a watering schedule is not a hard fast rule, it will help you to better monitor your plants. Remember that with the more intense summer sun you may need to increase watering for your windowsill friends and gradually adjust as the seasons change.

Soil Type: Depending on plant type, potting soil needs may differ. The most common type of potting soil is an "all purpose" type containing proportions of peat moss or coir fiber (a by-product of coconut), perlite (harder volcanic rock white in color) or vermiculite (softer silicate material beige in color), limestone (to neutralize pH), sand, and orchid bark. Inorganic materials such as sand, pumice or perlite help with drainage, aeration to the roots and moisture retention, while organic matter such as sphagnum peat moss, compost, vermiculite, orchid bark, and coir fiber help to not only aerate the soil but also add essential nutrients. Note that an outdoor potting mix generally contains greater amounts of fertilizer and moisture-controlling pellets, making it much too dense for houseplants. While most plants grow well in an all-purpose mix, cacti and succulents prefer a higher content in sand while orchids and bromeliads do best in orchid bark.

IDENTIFICATION OF SOIL COMPONENTS:

FIGURE 1: ALL PURPOSE MIX

FIGURE 4: ORCHID BARK

FIGURE 2: PERLITE

FIGURE 5: SPHAGNUM MOSS

FIGURE 3: VERMICULITE

FIGURE 6: SAND

Soil Type Recipes: A large percentage of houseplants are referred to as Aroids, or plant members from the family Araceae, which includes many common houseplants such as Monsteras, Chinese Evergreen, Philodendrons, Pothos and ZZ plants. Aroids generally prefer an organic soil with good drainage, so a soil mixture of 30% general potting soil, 40% orchid bark, 20% coco coir and 10% perlite suits them well. Moisture-loving plants such as Boston Fern, Bird's Nest Fern and Peace Lily prefer a slightly denser soil

6

mixture, which consists of 50% general potting soil, 30% orchid bark and 20% perlite. Mixing in two tablespoons of horticultural charcoal will help with the absorption of any excess moisture, while preventing damage to roots. In the case of succulents such as Thanksgiving Cactus, Snake Plant and Haworthia, a soil mixture of 50% general potting soil, 20% orchid bark, 20% horticultural sand and 10% perlite for drainage is preferred, while Hoya grow best in a mixture of 10% general potting soil, 40% cocoa coir, 30% orchid bark and 20% perlite, providing excellent drainage and needed air flow around the roots. These soil mixes can be purchased pre-made or you can have fun creating your own ideal mix! When mixing your soil, 10% would be equivalent to one scoop, 20% equal to two scoops of the same size, and so forth. Add increased proportional amounts of each ingredient to satisfy the size of your planter. Do note that Tillandsia are air plants and should not be grown in soil. They grow happily perched on a piece of bark, in a bed of gravel, or displayed in shells.

Feeding: Houseplants require macro and micronutrients to survive. To keep your houseplants healthy, feed them approximately once a month during the growing season (early spring to late summer) with an all-purpose slow-release balanced plant food with equal percentages of macronutrients nitrogen, phosphorus, and potassium. I tend to use slow-release plant foods because of their ability to release nutrients in smaller amounts over a longer period, hence being healthier for the plant. Flowering plants, such as African Violet, Peace Lily, Anthurium and Orchids require a plant food containing a higher percentage of phosphorus to promote blooms. Avoid fertilizing over the winter months when plants are not active and do not fertilize too often, as it can do more harm than good.

Humidity: Many species of plants, such as ferns, bromeliads, Ponytail Palm and Money Tree thrive in higher humidity and often require twenty to forty percent more humidity than is found in our homes. Signs of stress from low humidity include browning of the edges and tips of foliage, then followed by yellowing and crispy leaves. To increase humidity levels around your plants, set up a pebble tray beneath the planter filled with water, so that the water can evaporate up and around the plant. Use a larger tray than the bottom of the plant and fill with just enough water to barely cover the pebbles. The pebbles will keep the pot above water so that the roots are not constantly wet. Another method is to occasionally spritz the foliage with filtered or distilled water when sunlight is not beating directly on the plant. Surrounding the plant with sphagnum moss also helps to hold in moisture and humidity. Try to keep your humidity-loving plants away from heat sources, doorways, or areas where drafts can decrease moisture.

Purchasing & Potting Your Plants: When buying your plants and bringing them home for the first time, be sure to inspect for any browning, spots, or signs of disease. When you get your plants home and are ready to repot them, choose a planter which is only slightly larger than the planter it came in and check the roots to see their condition. Place soil in the bottom of the pot and be sure that the top of the soil of your new plant is in line with the rim of the pot. This is important to allow the roots room to grow and to prevent watering issues down the road. If the plant is rootbound (meaning the roots are tightly squeezed into the space and wrapped around the plant), use your fingers to slightly loosen up the roots. If they are severely root bound, you may need to take a scissor or razor blade and gently cut the bottom section of root so that they are able to spread out over time and take in nutrients. When potting, be sure there is a hole for drainage in the bottom. If not, you may have to use a drill bit to create one. A smaller pot should only need one drainage hole, while larger pots (twelve inches and up) may need several.

Potting Materials: There are several potting materials to choose from but do keep in mind that different plants have varying preferences. Types of materials for containers include terracotta, ceramic or glazed, concrete or stone, plastic, resin, metal, and wood. Succulents and cacti such as Aloe Vera, Echeveria, Jade Plant, and Barrel Cactus prefer a dry, well-drained soil and do best in a porous planter such as terracotta or concrete. This material allows excess moisture to escape and the soil to dry out faster. For a more modern look, a metal planter is suitable for succulents, cacti and some herbs like Rosemary and Thyme. Do keep in mind however that metal can heat up and that the planter should be kept within reasonable proximity from direct sun. For a touch of whimsy in your decor, you may choose one of the many succulent planters (Figure 7) that are available on the market! For tropical plants such as Rattlesnake Plant, Peace Lily, Prayer Plant, Pothos, Philodendron and Spider Plant, which prefer more consistent moisture, the usage of ceramic, glazed or plastic pots is best. These containers lack the ability for air to move through them, in return keeping the soil moist.

FIGURE 7: FAUX TREE LOG SUCCULENT PLANTER

For orchids, the use of a specialized orchid pot designed with slits for good drainage and proper air circulation around the plant's roots is recommended. The opposite is true of Lucky Bamboo, which thrives best in a closed ceramic container containing pebbles and water to support the bamboo's hydroponic growth. If it is a more rustic look you are hoping for, wooden planters can be used for plants that prefer a well-drained soil and slightly higher moisture levels. Examples include ferns, orchids, and certain varieties of philodendrons. Keep in mind your plant's needs while selecting a planter.

Decorating with Houseplants: Decorating and designing with houseplants can be a fun and creative art, while improving your mood and supplying a healthy environment. There are several ways to enhance your space and accomplish a beautiful and inviting look. For starters, save floor space and add a vertical accent by placing cascading or trailing plants including Pothos, Spider Plant, Tradescantia, String of Pearls, Ivy, or Boston Fern into hanging pots suspended from the ceiling with perhaps a decorative macrame hanger.

To add some interest to a bedroom, kitchen, or workspace, place groupings of plants on a windowsill to take advantage of natural light and add a lovely touch of green. If you have limited space or lighting or are simply looking for decorating ideas, there are also numerous types of benches, shelving units and plant stands of varying heights and dimensions to create a dynamic and organized display. Some plant stands even come equipped with built-in grow lights to address your lighting needs while adding a touch of decor to your space.

Another option is to cluster plants in a corner to maximize space or display plants in wall mounted pots to create a living wall. If you have an electric fireplace try adding plants to give it a cozier touch. For your succulents or air plants, terrariums or glass bulbs can be used to create a miniature ecosystem.

For your bathroom or kitchen where low light and high humidity conditions exist, add plants such as Snake Plant, ZZ plant, ferns, or Lucky Bamboo.

Use your imagination and get as creative as you like when displaying your green friends. Remember to mix and match plants with similar lighting, soil and moisture needs to create a diverse and visually appealing indoor garden. Here are some ideas to get you started. The possibilities are endless!

Chapter 1: Houseplant Profiles A-Z

From a young age, I have had a passion for houseplants. I believe the reason is because they add an element of life and beauty to the home. Perhaps it was out of a need to nurture or a desire to extend the outdoors inside. My collection of greenery has varied over the past forty years, with most plants contained within the main plant room, and the remaining scattered throughout other rooms of the house. These days I generally average about forty houseplants at a time and enjoy each one for its unique characteristics and growth habits. For informational purposes, I have either personally grown or have connections with someone who has grown each plant I bring to you. Each selection is listed alphabetically first by common name, followed by botanical name, information on lighting and soil moisture needs, humidity requirements if needed, and pet friendliness. When it comes to pet friendliness, if a plant is listed as pet friendly, it means that the plant is non-toxic, and will not cause harm, or irritation if ingested. Do note that while the plant is considered safe, some pets may be more sensitive or prone to mid stomach upset. If unsure, it is advisable to keep plants out of your pet's reach. In addition to the above, other notable tips about each plant will be included in its description, while in later chapters, plant maintenance tips will be provided to help ensure the health of your indoor garden.

For reference, there are basic categories of houseplants, including, but not limited to foliage plants, flowering plants, succulents, cacti and epiphytes, air purifiers, climbing or trailing plants, pet-friendly plants, and low maintenance plants. Foliage plants such as Spider Plant, Ferns, Monstera, Pothos, Calathea, Philodendron, Fiddle Leaf Fig, Alocasia, and Palms are known for their attractive foliage while flowering plants such as orchids, Peace Lily, Begonia, Anthurium, Kalanchoe and African Violet are prized for their ability to produce colorful and often fragrant blooms.

Succulents such as Aloe Vera, Jade Plant, Haworthia and Echeveria possess thick, fleshy leaves or roots adapted to store moisture, while Epiphytes are plants which naturally grow on other surfaces but are uniquely adapted to absorb moisture and nutrients from the air, rather than depending on soil. Examples of Epiphytes include Orchids, Bromeliads, and Tillandsia Xerographica among other varieties. Perhaps incorporate these into an amazing living wall!

Houseplants including African Violet, Boston Fern, Spider Plants, and Snake Plant are considered air purifiers, as they improve air quality by removing certain toxins while releasing oxygen. Climbing or trailing plants produce downward stems which are suitable for hanging planters. Philodendron, Tradescantia, String of Pearls, Pothos and Spider Plant fit this category. Examples of pet friendly plants include Parlor Palm, Ponytail Palm, African Violet, and Spider Plant. An extremely popular request is for houseplants considered to be low maintenance. These include, but are not limited to Parlor Palm, Snake Plant, Pothos, Jade and ZZ Plant. These plants require minimal care, are more resilient to variations in lighting and moisture, and have greater adaptability to indoor conditions.

Whatever your preference or lifestyle, there is a wide variety of houseplants from which you can choose. Whether you prefer low maintenance, drought tolerance, colorful blooms, outstanding foliage, pet friendliness or perhaps air-purifying qualities, there is likely to be a houseplant that is right for you!

COMMON NAME: AFRICAN VIOLET
BOTANICAL NAME: SAINTPAULIA IONANTHA
LIGHTING REQUIREMENTS: BRIGHT INDIRECT
SOIL MOISTURE NEEDS: MODERATE, WATER FROM BOTTOM
PET FRIENDLY: YES

African Violet is one of the most popular houseplants for a variety of reasons including vibrant blooms, easy care, and air purifying abilities. It needs between 10 to 12 hours of sunlight and 8 hours of darkness to flower, and thrives on humidity, so placement in a bright location with indirect or filtered light such as a kitchen or bathroom is ideal. Grouping plants together or providing a pebble tray partially filled with water can also create the same effect. Use distilled room temperature water and water from the bottom as it is important to keep the leaves dry. African Violet prefer to be semi rootbound, so for an average plant a four-to-six-inch planter is ideal. Feed with a water-soluble plant food at half strength every four to six weeks during the growing season.

COMMON NAME: AIR PLANT
BOTANICAL NAME: TILLANDSIA
LIGHTING REQUIREMENTS: BRIGHT INDIRECT
MOISTURE NEEDS: MODERATE, REQUIRES HIGH HUMIDITY
PET FRIENDLY: YES

Tillandsia is a genus of about 650 species of epiphyte, meaning that they attach to other plants or substrate as a means of support. The roots are used solely for attachment and the plant obtains moisture and nutrients from the air using specialized trichomes in the leaves. Tillandsia grow between 2-12 inches tall, require bright indirect light, and thrive on humidity, making them ideal for kitchens and bathrooms. To maintain plants rinse or mist twice weekly with tepid water or submerge for 20 minutes to an hour weekly and lay face down to remove excess water, a method which I find to work best. Air Plants bloom once in a lifetime then produce small offshoots or pups that can be separated and grown on their own. Fertilize Tillandsia monthly with a fertilizer formulated for bromeliads.

COMMON NAME: ALOE (FAN)
BOTANICAL NAME: KUMARA PLICATILIS, FORMERLY ALOE PLICATILIS
LIGHTING REQUIREMENTS: BRIGHT
SOIL MOISTURE NEEDS: LOW
PET FRIENDLY: NO

Fan Aloe is an unusual and striking fan-like succulent that can grow as large as a multi-stemmed shrub or small tree. As a houseplant it is easy to grow, low maintenance and will not need repotting for two to five years as it does grow slowly. Locate Fan Aloe in a bright sunny window and pot in a well-drained potting soil. Water on the side of caution, every other week during the growing season and less in wintertime. This succulent will send out offsets over time that can be separated from the main plant and repotted. Another method is to propagate by cuttings. Use a sterile knife to get a stem, allow to callus over a day or two and plant in a well-drained soil. Fan Aloe produces spikes of orange-red tubular blooms from winter to spring when the conditions are right.

COMMON NAME: ALOE (LACE)
BOTANICAL NAME: ARISTALOE ARISTATA
LIGHTING REQUIREMENTS: BRIGHT
SOIL MOISTURE NEEDS: LOW
PET FRIENDLY: NO

Lace Aloe is a compact hardy succulent named for its lacy leaves adorned with white bumps speckled upon deep green foliage. It can grow to eight inches tall by six inches wide and will produce off shoots or pups over time which can be separated and planted. Lace Aloe thrives in a well-drained soil in a bright sunny spot such as a southern or western window and prefers to be underwatered over being overwatered. Water every two weeks during the growing season and less in winter and allow to dry out in between, as the thick fleshy stems store moisture for times of drought. In the perfect conditions Lace Aloe will produce stalks of tubular shaped orange flowers. During the growing season you can apply a balanced natural fertilizer once a year, but feed sparingly.

24

COMMON NAME: ALOE (MEDICINAL ALOE)
BOTANICAL NAME: ALOE VERA
LIGHTING REQUIREMENTS: BRIGHT
SOIL MOISTURE NEEDS: LOW
PET FRIENDLY: NO

Aloe Vera is a well-known plant valued for its medicinal and air purifying qualities. Common uses include topical treatment for sunburn, skin rashes, acne and use in hair conditioners. Aloe is low maintenance, only requires bright sunlight and will tolerate infrequent watering. Plant in a succulent mix with good drainage, place in a sunny window and water only when the soil feels dry to the touch. This plant thrives in limited growing space and can reach a height of three feet over time. To propagate, wait until the off shoots or "pups" are at least one fifth the size of the parent plant. Using a clean sharp knife separate the pups from the main plant and replant. Since Aloe does not require much fertilization, feeding once a year in spring with a balanced plant food will suffice.

COMMON NAME: ALOE (SPIRAL)
BOTANICAL NAME: ALOE POLYPHYLLA
LIGHTING REQUIREMENTS: BRIGHT INDIRECT
SOIL MOISTURE NEEDS: MODERATE
PET FRIENDLY: NO

Aloe Polyphylla or Spiral Aloe is a rare and beautiful succulent native to the Maluti Mountains in Lesotho, Africa and named for the way its thick green leaves are arranged in a compact symmetrical spiral going either clockwise or counterclockwise as the plant matures. This variety prefers to be grown in a loose well-drained, slightly acidic sandy soil with good aeration. Place in a location with bright indirect sunlight and water moderately during the growing season when the top layer of soil becomes dry. Spiral Aloe grow to a mature size of 12 inches tall by 24 inches wide and while blooming is rare, a mature plant may produce stalks of pinkish-orange flowers in springtime. Tip: Be patient, as the first leaves grow upward. Once the leaves start spiraling do not rotate the pot to maintain leaf symmetry.

COMMON NAME: ALWORTHIA 'BLACK GEM', ALOE 'BLACK GEM'
BOTANICAL NAME: ALWORTHIA PENTAGONA 'BLACK GEM'
LIGHTING REQUIREMENTS: BRIGHT INDIRECT
MOISTURE NEEDS: LOW
PET FRIENDLY: YES

Aloe 'Black Gem' is a succulent that has become quite popular among plant enthusiasts. Formed from a cross between Aloe speciosa and Haworthia cymbiformis, this easy-care plant grows to six to eight inches and produces rosettes of thick fleshy green triangular stems that deepen to reddish brown or bronze in higher light. For healthy growth, pot this plant in a well-draining succulent or all-purpose potting mix and place in bright, but indirect light, avoiding direct light as it can scorch the leaves. I find a western exposure windowsill to be ideal. To prevent root rot, allow the top layer of soil to dry out before rewatering. Propagation is easy through off shoots and in the right conditions, small tubular flowers ranging in color from pale pink to coral may surprise you in the summer months!

COMMON NAME: AMARYLLIS
BOTANICAL NAME: HIPPEASTRUM
LIGHTING REQUIREMENTS: BRIGHT
SOIL MOISTURE NEEDS: MODERATE
PET FRIENDLY: NO

Amaryllis is a popular houseplant for the winter months with its large showy blooms available in a variety of colors that last for four to eight weeks. Plant the bulb one quarter to halfway exposed in a rich humus soil and keep moderately moist in a sunny window. Avoid watering the portion of the bulb that is exposed above the soil and feed with a balanced fertilizer once or twice a month. Amaryllis bulbs need eight to ten weeks of dormancy to rebloom. After blooming, allow the foliage to remain to build strength back into the bulb. Once the foliage dies back remove the bulb, allow it to dry out, and store it in a cool dry location until the next season. Start forcing bulbs 6-8 weeks before desired blooms watering sparingly until the bulb starts to sprout, then water weekly afterwards and enjoy!

COMMON NAME: ANTHURIUM, FLAMINGO FLOWER, LACELEAF
BOTANICAL NAME: ANTHURIUM ANDRAEANUM
LIGHTING REQUIREMENTS: BRIGHT INDIRECT
SOIL MOISTURE NEEDS: MODERATE
PET FRIENDLY: NO

Anthurium display shiny dark green elongated heart-shaped leaves, and the flowers are really called inflorescences, which are accompanied by colorful bracts in shades of red, pink, rose, or white. Place anthurium in a warm, brightly lit room but out of direct sun. The brighter the indirect lighting the more flowers the plant will produce. Anthuriums do not like dry air, so be sure to keep the humidity surrounding the plant around eighty percent. This can be achieved using a pebble tray or humidifier. Water thoroughly until liquid flows through the bottom of the plant into a saucer and discard any extra water. Allow the top layer of the soil to dry out in between waterings, feed during the growing season with a diluted liquid fertilizer and prune off dead or dying foliage to keep your plant healthy.

COMMON NAME: ARALIA FABIAN STUMP
BOTANICAL NAME: POLYSCIAS SCUTELLARIA 'FABIAN'
LIGHTING REQUIREMENTS: BRIGHT INDIRECT OR MODERATE
SOIL MOISTURE NEEDS: MODERATE, AVOID OVERWATERING
PET FRIENDLY: NO, ALL PARTS ARE HARMFUL IF INGESTED

Fabian Aralia is a unique air purifying houseplant that grows to 3-4 foot tall and thrives in bright indirect sunlight away from intense rays. Give moderate to high humidity and allow the top inch of soil to dry out in between waterings. Remove suckers from the trunk to maintain their treelike appearance and avoid drafts, as it can cause the plant to lose leaves. Feed monthly during the growing season with general-purpose fertilizer at half strength. Note: Aralia may go through a slight dormancy in winter dropping some of its leaves to conserve energy. Reduce watering at that time and new growth will appear in spring. Avoid this plant around children and pets.

30

COMMON NAME: ARECA PALM (BAMBOO PALM)
BOTANICAL NAME: DYPSIS LUTESCENS
LIGHTING REQUIREMENTS: BRIGHT INDIRECT
SOIL MOISTURE NEEDS: MODERATE, PREFERS SLIGHTLY HIGHER HUMIDITY
PET FRIENDLY: YES

Areca Palm is a popular, easy-care houseplant with a slow to moderate growth rate, reaching a mature size of up to six to eight feet indoors. It prefers a warm location out of drafts and bright indirect lighting, as direct sunlight can scorch the leaves. The secret of success is to get the watering right. Palms prefer a well-drained peat based potting mix and soil that is moist but not constantly wet. Allow the top layer of soil to dry before rewatering. If the tips of leaves are turning brown, misting or use of a pebble tray can increase humidity. Under ideal conditions it is normal for Areca Palm to shed its older leaves. Remove completely browned fronds and feed regularly with a slow-release fertilizer higher in nitrogen and potassium during spring and summer to maintain the health of your plant.

COMMON NAME: ARROWHEAD PLANT
BOTANICAL NAME: SYNGONIUM PODOPHYLLUM
LIGHTING REQUIREMENTS: MEDIUM BRIGHT, INDIRECT SUN
SOIL MOISTURE NEEDS: MODERATE
PET FRIENDLY: NO

Native to the tropical rainforests of Central and South America, Arrowhead Plant is a popular houseplant known for its spade-like leaves and lush foliage ranging in a variety of colors and patterns from dark green with white variegation to hues of lime and pink. Locate this plant in medium to bright light, avoiding direct sun. Provide moderate moisture, allowing the soil to dry out slightly between waterings. Once mature, Syngonium podophyllum reaches approximately fifteen inches tall and is frequently used as a trailing plant that can be trained to grow up a pole for added interest. To maintain a fuller more compact plant, remove climbing stems that develop and pinch back new growth. Apply a balanced fertilizer during the growing season to keep your plant healthy and vibrant.

COMMON NAME: ASPARAGUS FERN
BOTANICAL NAME: ASPARAGUS DENSIFLORUS 'MYERSII'
LIGHTING REQUIREMENTS: BRIGHT INDIRECT
SOIL MOISTURE NEEDS: MODERATE, PREFERS SLIGHTLY HIGHER HUMIDITY
PET FRIENDLY: NO

Asparagus Fern is known for its attractive feathery light green foliage and easy care. Despite its name, it is not a true fern, but rather a member of Asparagaceae family. It thrives in indirect light and a slightly humid environment, making it excellent for growing in kitchens, bathrooms or moved to a shaded location outdoors during the summer months. Plant Asparagus Fern in a location with bright indirect sun in an organically rich, well-drained soil and keep it evenly moist. Trim back stem tips every few months to maintain denser growth. Group Asparagus Fern with other plantings, mist occasionally or use a pebble tray to supply the humidity it thrives on. Asparagus Fern is a tuberous evergreen perennial, can grow to one to two feet tall by three to four foot wide and is easily propagated by division.

COMMON NAME: BEGONIA
BOTANICAL NAME: BEGONIA REX
LIGHTING REQUIREMENTS: MEDIUM TO BRIGHT, INDIRECT
SOIL MOISTURE NEEDS: MODERATE, BUT NOT WET, WATER FROM BOTTOM
PET FRIENDLY: NO

Rex Begonia is a popular houseplant grown mostly for its showy foliage followed by dainty blooms on a 12-24 inch tall by wide plant, with many cultivars available. Begonia prefers medium to bright indirect lighting such as an eastern facing window and evenly moist well-drained soil. Avoid placing in direct sunlight as it will burn the tender leaves and allow the soil to dry partially between waterings. To encourage plant health and blooms, feed during spring and summer with a balanced liquid fertilizer at half strength during alternate waterings. Since Begonia do not like water on their leaves, avoid misting, and bottom watering is encouraged. Begonia are an easy-care houseplant but do note that they have a lifespan of approximately two to three years.

They can be propagated by cuttings or division. Other popular varieties for foliage include Begonia Rex Escargot (Figure 1) and Begonia Rex Red Escargot (Figure 2).

FIGURE 1: BEGONIA REX ESCARGOT

FIGURE 2: BEGONIA REX RED ESCARGOT

COMMON NAME: BIRD OF PARADISE
BOTANICAL NAME: STRELITZIA REGINAE
LIGHTING REQUIREMENTS: BRIGHT, INDIRECT
SOIL MOISTURE NEEDS: MODERATE, WELL-DRAINED
ADDITIONAL: PREFERS HIGH HUMIDITY
PET FRIENDLY: NO

If you want to bring a little bit of the tropics to your space, Bird of Paradise displays lush fan-like leaves and colorful orange, blue and purple bird-like blooms on a 3-5 foot tall by wide plant when grown in the perfect conditions. Flowering is rare and considered a treat when indoors, but some gardeners find that by reducing water or increasing lights for a short period of time while fertilizing in spring and summer can stimulate blooms. Place Bird of Paradise in a bright location with at least four hours of southern or western exposure and water every one to two weeks, allowing the soil to dry halfway between waterings. Bird of Paradise prefers humidity, which can be provided by a humidifier or pebble tray with water.

COMMON NAME: BIRD'S NEST FERN
BOTANICAL NAME: ASPLENIUM NIDUS
LIGHTING REQUIREMENTS: FILTERED SUNLIGHT TO PARTIAL SHADE
SOIL MOISTURE NEEDS: MODERATE, BUT NOT WET
ADDITIONAL: PREFERS HIGH HUMIDITY
PET FRIENDLY: YES. NOT TOXIC, BUT CAN CAUSE TEMPORARY MILD
IRRITATION

A popular houseplant for filtered sunlight to partial shade, Bird's Nest Fern are epiphytic in nature and grow to two feet tall by wide indoors. They display smooth, lance-shaped fronds that emerge from a central rosette and develop gentle ripples in the correct lighting. Ideal in an eastern or northern facing exposure, these plants thrive in a soil that is loose and rich in organic matter with excellent drainage. Water from soil level to avoid wetting the delicate fronds and provide consistent moisture but avoid soggy soil. Ferns prefer higher humidity and moist environments making them ideal for a bathroom, greenhouse, or terrarium. They enjoy a feeding during the growing season with a balanced liquid fertilizer at half strength.

COMMON NAME: BOSTON FERN OR SWORD FERN
BOTANICAL NAME: NEPHROLEPIS EXALTATA
LIGHTING REQUIREMENTS: BRIGHT INDIRECT
SOIL MOISTURE NEEDS: MOIST
ADDITIONAL: PREFERS HIGH HUMIDITY
PET FRIENDLY: YES

Boston Fern are known for their feathery arching fronds and love of humidity. They are best placed in indirect bright light such as near a window with filtered lighting or in a location with dappled shade. Keep their soil consistently moist but not waterlogged and supply the humidity they require by placing them in a kitchen or bathroom or by making use of a pebble tray. Frequent misting also prevents the foliage from drying out. Boston Fern prefer a rich, well-drained potting mix containing peat to retain moisture and being fed with a balanced liquid fertilizer at half strength during the growing season. Prune regularly to remove any dead or yellowing foliage to keep your plant healthy and to promote new growth.

COMMON NAME: BROMELIAD, PINEAPPLE PLANT
BOTANICAL NAME: BROMELIACEAE GUZMANIA
LIGHTING REQUIREMENTS: BRIGHT INDIRECT
SOIL MOISTURE NEEDS: WELL DRAINED
ADDITIONAL: PREFERS HIGH HUMIDITY
PET FRIENDLY: YES

Bromeliads are relatively easy to care for and make stunning houseplants. Grow in a loose soil containing orchid bark to allow for air circulation and place in a location with bright indirect light. Water in the central cup, allowing it to drain every few days and allow the surrounding top inch of soil to dry in between waterings. To maintain humidity, mist regularly or place the plant on a tray with pebbles and water. Bromeliads are light feeders. It is best to use a diluted fertilizer and either lightly mist the leaves or apply directly to the soil. Most bromeliads bloom only once in their lifetime, but the colorful bracts can last for months. Once the mother plant produces pups they can be separated and replanted to form new plants.

COMMON NAME: BURRO'S TAIL OR DONKEY'S TAIL
BOTANICAL NAME: SEDUM MORGANIANUM
LIGHTING REQUIREMENTS: BRIGHT LIGHT
SOIL MOISTURE NEEDS: LOW
PET FRIENDLY: NO

Displaying light green foliage and trailing stems, Burro's Tail, or Donkey's Tail is a slow growing succulent which can be displayed alone as a hanging plant or perhaps paired with other succulents in a dish garden. Plant in a well-draining cactus or succulent mix, provide bright, indirect sunlight, and water sparingly, allowing the soil to dry out completely in between waterings. As the plant grows and stems become long (up to 2-4 feet) and heavy, a stake or trellis can be used for support, or the plant can be allowed to cascade freely. If leaves fall off, they can be easily propagated placed on top of a well-draining soil, eventually forming roots to create new plants. Succulents are not heavy feeders. Feed with a water-soluble balanced fertilizer once a month during spring and summer.

COMMON NAME: CACTUS (CALIFORNIA BARREL CACTUS)
BOTANICAL NAME: FEROCACTUS CYLINDRACEUS
LIGHTING REQUIREMENTS: BRIGHT, DIRECT
SOIL MOISTURE NEEDS: LOW
PET FRIENDLY: NO

Barrel Cactus is a slow growing spherical cactus native to regions of southwestern America. As a mature houseplant it can reach one to two feet tall over time and has sharp, colorful spines that help to reduce water loss and range in color from yellow to red. In ideal conditions, this species of Barrel Cactus may produce yellow flowers that grow as a ring at the top of the plant. This low maintenance plant requires bright direct sun, as from a western or southern window, well-draining soil, and infrequent watering. Water every 2-3 weeks during the growing season and reduce in wintertime, always allowing the soil to dry out in between waterings. Feed your Barrel Cactus once a month only during the growing season with a diluted, low nitrogen cactus fertilizer. Wear gloves when handling!

COMMON NAME: CACTUS (BLUE COLUMNAR OR BLUE TORCH)
BOTANICAL NAME: PILOSOCEREUS PACHYCLADUS
LIGHTING REQUIREMENTS: BRIGHT
SOIL MOISTURE NEEDS: LOW
PET FRIENDLY: NO

As with other members of the cacti family, Pilosocereus is a low maintenance houseplant requiring plenty of direct sunlight and minimal watering. Grow this more upright, columnar cacti in a well-draining cactus or succulent mix, place in a southern or western window with at least six hours of light, and water only when the top inch of soil feels dry to the touch. During winter, this plant will go into dormancy, so even less watering is needed at that time. Since cacti prefer dry air and warmer temperatures between 65 to 85 degrees Fahrenheit (18 to 27 degrees Celsius), avoid placing near cold drafts that could stress the plant. Fertilize with a balanced low nitrogen fertilizer at half strength during the growing season and repot your plant every two to three years or when the plant outgrows its space.

COMMON NAME: CACTUS (GRAFTED)
BOTANICAL NAME: GYMNOCALYCIUM MIHANOVICHII
LIGHTING REQUIREMENTS: BRIGHT INDIRECT
SOIL MOISTURE NEEDS: LOW
PET FRIENDLY: NO

Grafted cacti bring interest to the indoor garden with an additional touch of color and style. Grafting creates a unique hybrid with a combination of desirable traits by attaching a more colorful top portion (the scion) to the main bottom portion (the rootstock). This process not only helps to preserve rare or endangered species but creates a relationship in which the top plant uses the nutrients and energy from the bottom portion to help it grow more vigorously than it would on its own. Keep grafted cacti in bright indirect light, as the brightly colored scion is more prone to sunburn. Water sparingly and use a well-draining cactus or succulent mix. A blend that includes sand, perlite and potting soil will help prevent water retention; thus, keeping the rootstock healthy.

COMMON NAME: CALATHEA FASCIATA
BOTANICAL NAME: GOEPPERTIA FASCIATA
LIGHTING REQUIREMENTS: BRIGHT INDIRECT
SOIL MOISTURE NEEDS: MODERATE, WELL-DRAINED
PET FRIENDLY: YES

Calathea fasciata is known for its attractive broad, green foliage highlighted with darker patterns. Grow this beauty in bright indirect light, avoiding direct sunlight, as it can scorch the leaves. It is best to water with filtered or distilled water as Calathea are sensitive to chlorine and fluoride. Plant in a well-draining peat based potting mix, keep the soil consistently moist but not wet, and water when the top one to two inches of soil feels dry to the touch. Calathea thrive in high humidity and prefer temperatures between 65 to 80 degrees Fahrenheit (18 to 27 degrees Celsius), so avoid putting in a location where it can be subject to drafts. Feed with a balanced fertilizer once a month during the growing season and remove any yellowing or damaged leaves to keep the plant looking its best.

COMMON NAME: CALATHEA WHITESTAR
BOTANICAL NAME: CALATHEA MAJESTICA
LIGHTING REQUIREMENTS: BRIGHT INDIRECT
SOIL MOISTURE NEEDS: MODERATE, WELL-DRAINED
PET FRIENDLY: YES

Calathea Whitestar is a striking variety of Calathea displaying elongated leaves adorned with white, green, and pink stripes along with purplish undersides. It has the same requirements as other Calathea but can be a little challenging due to the delicate nature of its leaves. Grow in a well-drained peat-based plant mix with good aeration in bright, indirect light, while keeping the soil consistently moist, but not wet. This plant prefers higher humidity and should be watered with filtered or distilled water to avoid damage. Fertilize during the growing season with a balanced liquid fertilizer at half strength and watch for insects especially under the leaves. If spotted, remove the affected part, and avoid using strong insecticides which can burn the plant. Neem oil or mild dish soap is best.

COMMON NAME: CAST IRON PLANT
BOTANICAL NAME: ASPIDISTRA ELATIOR
LIGHTING REQUIREMENTS: LOW TO MEDIUM INDIRECT
SOIL MOISTURE NEEDS: MODERATE, WELL DRAINED
PET FRIENDLY: YES

Low maintenance and easy to care for, Cast Iron Plant prefer low to medium indirect light and are drought tolerant, but prefer consistent moisture. Plant in a well-draining potting mix and water when the top inch of soil feels dry to the touch. Known for its durability and long, lance-shaped leaves that grow upright, Cast Iron Plant is excellent for low light indoor spaces such as offices, entryways, and rooms with little natural light. They grow slowly, reaching about two to three feet in height and their clumping nature makes them excellent for filling in spaces. While the leaves on this cultivar are deep green, there are other varieties displaying variegated leaves with broad yellow or white stripes. Cat Iron Plant does not require high humidity but can benefit from an occasional misting.

46

COMMON NAME: CAT PALM
BOTANICAL NAME: CHAMAEDOREA CATARACTARUM
LIGHTING REQUIREMENTS: BRIGHT INDIRECT
SOIL MOISTURE NEEDS: MODERATE, WELL DRAINED
ADDITIONAL: PREFERS HIGH HUMIDITY
PET FRIENDLY: YES

Cat Palm is known for its air purifying properties and lush, tropical appearance as it displays dense, feathery fronds with narrow green leaflets. This plant typically reaches between three to six feet, exhibiting a clumping nature with multiple stems from the base rather than a single trunk. Grow Cat Palm in bright, indirect light such as in a well-lit room and avoid direct sunlight., as it can scorch the leaves. Use a well-draining potting mix designed for palms or tropical plants and keep the soil consistently moist, but not wet. Cat Palm do prefer higher humidity levels, which can be accomplished through misting or use of a pebble tray. While Cat Plam are relatively pest resistant, wiping down the fronds with soapy water can help.

COMMON NAME: CHINESE EVERGREEN (GREEN)
BOTANICAL NAME: AGLAONEMA 'SILVER BAY'
LIGHTING REQUIREMENTS: MEDIUM TO LOW INDIRECT
SOIL MOISTURE NEEDS: MODERATE, WELL DRAINED
PET FRIENDLY: NO

Chinese Evergreen is a popular low maintenance houseplant known for its beautiful oval shaped variegated foliage that can range from shades of green to silver, cream, pink or red, depending on the variety. Grow in medium to low indirect lighting and water when the top one to two inches of soil are dry. This plant can tolerate low light but may grow more slowly or lose some of its variegation. Chinese Evergreen prefers a well-draining potting mix, moderate humidity, and thrives in temperatures between 65 to 80 degrees F (18 to 27 degrees C). A mature plant will grow to approximately one to three feet tall and can be propagated through division or stem cuttings. Fertilize every four to six weeks during the growing season. Chinese evergreen also plays a role in improving air quality.

COMMON NAME: CHINESE EVERGREEN (RED)
BOTANICAL NAME: AGLAONEMA 'JASPER JONES'
LIGHTING REQUIREMENTS: BRIGHT INDIRECT
SOIL MOISTURE NEEDS: MODERATE, WELL DRAINED
PET FRIENDLY: NO

This cultivar of Chinese Evergreen displays lush broad leaves in shades of red, pink, or deep reddish-pink hues, often paired with green or silvery markings. It prefers bright indirect light to maintain its vivid red coloration but should be kept out of direct light to prevent scorching. Like other Aglaonema, this variety of Chinese Evergreen prefers a well-draining soil and watering when the top one or two inches of soil become dry. Known for its air purifying properties by filtering toxins, this cultivar enjoys higher humidity and warm temperatures like its counterparts. Plant in a well-draining planting mix containing peat and perlite and fertilize every six to eight weeks during the growing season. Aglaonema 'Jasper Jones' grows to a size of one to three feet tall by wide at maturity.

COMMON NAME: CHINESE MONEY PLANT
BOTANICAL NAME: PILEA PEPEROMIOIDES
LIGHTING REQUIREMENTS: BRIGHT INDIRECT
SOIL MOISTURE NEEDS: MODERATE, WELL DRAINED
PET FRIENDLY: YES

The Chinese Money Plant is a popular easy-care houseplant known for its unique rounded, coin-like leaves growing on long stems, giving it an almost whimsical appearance. Native to the Yunnan Province in southern China, it is often associated with good luck, wealth, and prosperity. Due to its clumping nature and mature size of just twelve inches in height, this plant is perfect for small spaces. Grow in bright, indirect light in a well-draining potting mix and allow the top one inch of soil to dry out in between waterings. Note: Money Plant does not like to sit in water. Pilea peperomioides is known for producing pups that can be separated from the mother plant and shared once they have a few leaves of their own. Feed monthly with a balanced fertilizer at half strength during the growing season.

COMMON NAME: CHRISTMAS CACTUS
BOTANICAL NAME: SCHLUMBERGERA BRIDGESII
LIGHTING REQUIREMENTS: BRIGHT LIGHT
SOIL MOISTURE NEEDS: LOW
PET FRIENDLY: YES

Christmas cactus (Schlumbergera bridgesii) when compared to Thanksgiving cactus has more scalloped, or tear-drop shaped leaves and blooms closer to Christmas time and extending into January, while Thanksgiving cactus foliage is more jagged with a sharper claw-like look. Grow Christmas cactus in a southern or western location, such as a windowsill, where cooler winter temperatures trigger blooming. Water every 1-2 weeks when the top third of the soil is dry, reduce in fall before blooms and remove faded flowers to encourage more blooms. As new growth appears in spring, apply a weak strength fertilizer every 2-3 weeks, and pinch back leggy branches to keep fullness. The most common variety in nurseries is Thanksgiving Cactus but you may be fortunate to find this variety later in the season.

COMMON NAME: CLIVIA, NATAL LILY
BOTANICAL NAME: CLIVIA MINIATA
LIGHTING REQUIREMENTS: BRIGHT INDIRECT
SOIL MOISTURE NEEDS: MODERATE, WELL-DRAINED
PET FRIENDLY: NO

Clivia, commonly known as Natal Lily, displays dark green elongated leaves with clusters of slightly fragrant orange blooms with yellow centers which last for several weeks. Rarer cultivars include variegated or green foliage with yellow, peach, or white blooms. Clivia grows 18-24 inches in height, prefers bright indirect light, moderate watering, and a coarse well-drained soil, such as an orchid mix. To induce blooming, allow your plant to become slightly rootbound and reduce watering in fall. Placing the plant near a window mimics the cooling period needed for them to bloom. Blooms can occur twice a year, with the first bloom in late winter to early spring. After flowering remove flower stalks to push energy back into the plant and fertilize once a month during the growing season.

COMMON NAME: CORN PLANT
BOTANICAL NAME: DRACAENA FRAGRANS 'MASSANGEANA'
LIGHTING REQUIREMENTS: BRIGHT INDIRECT
SOIL MOISTURE NEEDS: MODERATE, WELL DRAINED
PET FRIENDLY: NO

The Corn Plant (Dracaena fragrans) is a popular and easy-care houseplant known for its lush arching green leaves with yellow accents and tropical-like appearance. It prefers a well-draining potting mix, evenly moist soil, and a location with bright indirect lighting, such as an eastern facing window, but it can tolerate lower light, making it more versatile for various rooms. Corn Plant does enjoy moderate to high humidity levels and is susceptible to cold drafts and temperature fluctuations. It can be sensitive to overwatering, which can lead to root rot, so allow the top layer of soil to dry between waterings. This cultivar is relatively maintenance free and easy to monitor. Brown leaf tips indicate low humidity or fluoride in tap water and leaf yellowing can be a sign of overwatering, while leaf drop often suggests underwatering or a sudden change in temperature or lighting. To keep your plant vibrant and healthy, feed with a balanced liquid fertilizer diluted to half strength every four to six weeks during the growing season. Corn Plant generally grows to a height of four to six feet or up to ten feet indoors with optimal care. There are several varieties to choose from including the most popular Dracaena fragrans 'Massangeana' with green leaves and wide yellow strip down the center and Dracaena 'Lemon Lime' (Figure 1) with vibrant green leaves with yellow and lime-colored edges.

FIGURE 1: DRACAENA FRAGRANS 'LEMON LIME'

COMMON NAME: CORN PLANT
BOTANICAL NAME: DRACAENA DEREMENSIS 'JANET CRAIG'
LIGHTING REQUIREMENTS: BRIGHT INDIRECT
SOIL MOISTURE NEEDS: MODERATE, WELL DRAINED
PET FRIENDLY: NO

Dracaena 'Janet Craig' is another beloved houseplant in the Dracaena family, valued for its compact habit and striking deep green foliage and air purifying properties. It thrives in low to moderate indirect light, making it ideal for office settings. Place this plant near a window or door in a well-lit spot using a well-draining soil with good aeration and water when the top inch of soil feels dry to the touch. Use a pot with excellent drainage, because as with other Dracaena, they do not like their roots to be constantly wet. Average humidity is generally sufficient, but if tips of leaves show signs of browning, supply a pebble tray, or lightly mist the leaves. Indoors, Dracaena 'Janet Craig' is slow growing and can reach a potential height of between two to five feet tall over time, making it perfect for smaller spaces.

COMMON NAME: CROTON PETRA
BOTANICAL NAME: CODIAEUM VARIEGATUM
LIGHTING REQUIREMENTS: BRIGHT INDIRECT
SOIL MOISTURE NEEDS: MODERATE, WELL DRAINED
PET FRIENDLY: NO

Croton Petra is a popular houseplant for its lush bright colorful foliage featuring shades of red, yellow, orange, and green. They prefer bright indirect sun as near an eastern, southern, or western window with 4-6 hours of indirect sun to keep the foliage colorful and vibrant. Keep the soil moderately moist, allowing it to slightly dry out in between waterings, but avoid prolonged periods of drought. To maintain proper humidity, use of a pebble tray or misting is recommended. Fading or scorching near the edges of leaves are signs of too much sunlight, while leaf shed is an indication of insufficient lighting. To keep your plant full, pinch off new leaves to encourage bushiness. As houseplants Croton Petra grow to 3-8 feet tall by 3-6 feet in width adding a tropical feel to your space.

COMMON NAME: CROTON 'GOLD DUST'
BOTANICAL NAME: CODIAEUM VARIEGATUM 'AUREO-MACULATUM'
LIGHTING REQUIREMENTS: BRIGHT INDIRECT
SOIL MOISTURE NEEDS: MODERATE, WELL DRAINED
PET FRIENDLY: NO

Croton 'Gold Dust' is another variety of Croton known for its deep green foliage speckled with bright yellow highlights resembling flecks of gold. Growing to ten feet tall in the wild, Croton 'Gold Dust' grows to approximately three feet high by wide as a houseplant and thrives in a brightly lit location in a well-drained soil with moderate watering, while allowing the soil to dry slightly in between watering. As with all Croton, supply adequate humidity and fertilize with a balanced liquid fertilizer every six to eight weeks during the growing season making sure the soil is slightly wet beforehand to avoid burning of roots. To encourage new growth prune back long or leggy stems in spring. Stem cuttings can be propagated using rooting hormone in soil but avoid getting the plant's sap on your skin.

COMMON NAME: CYCLAMEN, FLORIST CYCLAMEN
BOTANICAL NAME: CYCLAMEN PERSICUM
LIGHTING REQUIREMENTS: BRIGHT INDIRECT
SOIL MOISTURE NEEDS: MODERATE, WELL DRAINED, WATER FROM
BOTTOM
PET FRIENDLY: NO, EXTREMELY TOXIC

Florist, or indoor Cyclamen is popular for its large showy winter blooms in shades of pink, white, and red and often seen in garden centers during autumn through early spring. Grow Cyclamen in a cool bright spot such as in a conservatory, east or north facing windowsill and keep the soil moist, but not wet. Watering from the bottom is best, not allowing water to splash on the leaves. In spring, your Cyclamen will go into a dormant period and the leaves will start to die back. Stop watering the plant and locate it in a cool sheltered spot outside for the summer until new growth starts to appear in early fall. Bring the plant indoors, repot if needed and commence watering. Feed your Cyclamen every couple of months with a balanced fertilizer if you are planning to keep it from year to year.

COMMON NAME: DRAGON TREE
BOTANICAL NAME: DRACENA MARGINATA
LIGHTING REQUIREMENTS: BRIGHT INDIRECT
SOIL MOISTURE NEEDS: MODERATE, WELL DRAINED
PET FRIENDLY: NO

Dracaena marginata is known for its elegant, narrow spiky green leaves with reddish edges and tropical flair. Position in bright indirect light in a well-draining potting mix and water once the two inches of soil feel dry to the touch. Fertilize every four to six weeks during the growing season with a balanced liquid plant food. This cultivar can grow to a height of six feet or more indoors. Most Dracaena houseplants live up to ten to fifteen years when grown under optimal conditions.

COMMON NAME: DRAGON TREE
BOTANICAL NAME: DRACAENA MARGINATA 'COLORAMA'
LIGHTING REQUIREMENTS: BRIGHT INDIRECT
SOIL MOISTURE NEEDS: MODERATE, WELL DRAINED
PET FRIENDLY: NO

Dracaena marginata 'Colorama' is a popular houseplant for its vibrant pinkish-red margins, adding a pop of color. While Dracaena marginata can take slightly less light, 'Colorama' tends to need more lighting to maintain its bright color. With either plant avoid direct sun, as it can scorch the leaves. Both varieties are slow growing, not requiring frequent potting and are air purifiers, making them ideal for indoors. Dracaena 'Colorama' also grows to a mature height of six or more feet and maintains a width of approximately two to three feet. Both plants prefer average to slightly higher indoor humidity and are sensitive to excess moisture. The name Dragon Tree was derived partially from the plant's dragon-like qualities, such as its thick ridged trunk and spiky, sword-shaped leaves.

COMMON NAME: DUMB CANE
BOTANICAL NAME: DIEFFENBACHIA 'PANTHER'
LIGHTING REQUIREMENTS: BRIGHT INDIRECT
SOIL MOISTURE NEEDS: MODERATE, WELL DRAINED
PET FRIENDLY: NO, EXTREMELY TOXIC

Dumb Cane, or Dieffenbachia is an easy-care, moderately fast-growing houseplant known for its broad, oval shaped leaves with unique variegation. Depending on the species, it can grow between three and six feet tall indoors. This plant is toxic if ingested, causing irritation and swelling in the mouth and throat and is best kept away from pets and children. Grow in a well-draining peat-based soil in bright indirect light and water when the top one to two inches of soil are dry. Dumb Cane prefers moderate to high humidity, which can be supplied by misting or use of a pebble tray. Remove any yellowed or damaged leaves to encourage new growth and repot every one to two years to give the plant more room. There are several varieties to choose from varying in leaf size and variegation.

COMMON NAME: EASTER (SPRING) CACTUS
BOTANICAL NAME: RHIPSALIDOPSIS GAERTNERI 'SIRIUS'
LIGHTING REQUIREMENTS: BRIGHT LIGHT
SOIL MOISTURE NEEDS: LOW
PET FRIENDLY: YES

Rhipsalidopsis gaertneri, commonly known as Easter Cactus or Spring Cactus produces a profusion of star-shaped springtime flowers from March into May. Blooms last for weeks and open every morning after sunrise and close at sundown. In their native habitat, rhipsalidopsis grow as epiphytes in the forests of South America. Locate Easter Cactus in bright filtered light avoiding direct sunlight and grow in a well-drained soil with moderate watering. Apply a weak strength fertilizer every 2-3 weeks when buds form and pinch back leggy branches to encourage fullness. To extend the flowering season, keep plants cool and moist. The most common varieties of Easter Cactus are 'Sirius' (White), 'Columbia' (Orange), 'Scorpius' (Red) and 'Rosea' (Pink).

COMMON NAME: ELEPHANT EARS
BOTANICAL NAME: ALOCASIA 'POLLY'
LIGHTING REQUIREMENTS: BRIGHT INDIRECT
SOIL MOISTURE NEEDS: MODERATE, BUT NOT WET
PET FRIENDLY: NO

Alocasia 'Polly' is a compact hybrid known for its distinctive arrow shaped glossy deep green leaves with light creamy veining. Growing to 12-24 inches high by 10-12 inches wide, Alocasia 'Polly' performs best in an aroid soil mix in a warm location with bright indirect lighting, while keeping the soil lightly moist, but not wet. Alocasia do prefer humidity, so it is best to place it among other plants, near a humidifier or on a pebble tray with water. Alocasia are prone to spider mite, so cleaning the leaves with lukewarm water once or twice a year will help to prevent insect damage. Feed every two to four weeks with a diluted well-balanced fertilizer during the growing months and prune off occasional faded foliage to promote fullness and good health.

COMMON NAME: ELEPHANT EARS, TARO
BOTANICAL NAME: COLOCASIA ESCULENTA
LIGHTING REQUIREMENTS: BRIGHT INDIRECT
SOIL MOISTURE NEEDS: MODERATE, BUT NOT WET
PET FRIENDLY: NO

Colocasia esculenta, commonly known as Elephant Ears or Taro, is a tropical plant grown for its dramatic display of large heart shaped rich-green leaves which tend to point downward, unlike the deeper green more upward facing leaves of Alocasia. Growing to 3-6 feet tall by wide, this plant can be grown outside then brought indoors or can be grown as a houseplant all year long. Give it bright indirect lighting and keep the soil moderately moist, but not wet, and avoid placing the plant in full sun, as this will burn the leaves. Colocasia start to go dormant in temperatures below 21 degrees Celsius (69.8 F) and enjoy high humidity so placement in a bathroom, conservatory or greenhouse is ideal. Elephant Ear can be purchased as corms in springtime or as a full-grown plant later in the season.

COMMON NAME: ENGLISH IVY
BOTANICAL NAME: HEDERA HELIX
LIGHTING REQUIREMENTS: BRIGHT INDIRECT
SOIL MOISTURE NEEDS: MODERATE, WELL DRAINED
PET FRIENDLY: NO

Growing English Ivy indoors is quite simple to do and the benefits of its air purifying properties and trailing habit are rewarding. Locate this cascading plant in bright indirect light such as an eastern exposure or a couple of feet from a western facing window and keep the soil consistently moist but not wet. English Ivy thrives in cooler to average temperatures between 50 to 70 degrees Fahrenheit (10 to 21 Celsius) and appreciates higher humidity. Feed monthly spring through early fall with a balanced liquid fertilizer at half strength and prune regularly to maintain fullness and desired length. Remove any yellowing leaves and keep an eye out for common pests like spider mites, especially in drier conditions. If you notice pests, wash the leaves down with soapy water or insecticidal soap.

COMMON NAME: FALSE ARALIA
BOTANICAL NAME: PLERANDRA ELEGANTISSIMA
LIGHTING REQUIREMENTS: BRIGHT INDIRECT
SOIL MOISTURE NEEDS: MODERATE, BUT NOT WET
PET FRIENDLY: YES

False Aralia displays delicate, lacy foliage that adds a tropical feel to indoor spaces. Place False Aralia in bright, indirect light such as a few feet from a southern or western window and keep it away from cold drafts which can stress it. If your home is dry, consider a humidity tray or misting regularly. Provide a well-draining potting soil and water when the top one inch of soil feels dry. Prune any leggy growth to encourage fullness and feed with a balanced liquid fertilizer at half strength every four to six weeks during the growing season. This plant prefers to be slightly rootbound, so repotting is usually needed every two to three years. False Aralia is a bit sensitive to changes in environment, so avoid moving it frequently. With consistent care, it will reward you with its elegant foliage.

COMMON NAME: FICUS, GINGER FIG
BOTANICAL NAME: FICUS MICROCARPA 'GINSENG'
LIGHTING REQUIREMENTS: BRIGHT INDIRECT
SOIL MOISTURE NEEDS: MODERATE, WELL DRAINED
PET FRIENDLY: NO

Ginseng Ficus is known for its unique root structure and glossy foliage and often grown as an indoor bonsai. Locate Ginger Fig in a bright location with indirect sun, such as an eastern or northwestern window and water thoroughly when the top inch of soil is dry. Use a well-draining potting mix, preferably one formulated for bonsai or indoor trees with a mix of sand or perlite for drainage. Feed every four to six weeks during the growing season and prune regularly to maintain shape.

COMMON NAME: FIDDLE LEAF FIG
BOTANICAL NAME: FICUS LYRATA
LIGHTING REQUIREMENTS: BRIGHT INDIRECT
SOIL MOISTURE NEEDS: MODERATE, WELL DRAINED
PET FRIENDLY: NO

Fiddle Leaf Fig is known for its voluminous broad green leaves with distinct veining that add a lush tropical look to the home or office. As a houseplant, it grows between six and ten feet tall and thrives in a warm, humid environment with plenty of light. Fiddle Leaf Fig is sometimes described as "fickle" as it is not the easiest houseplant to take care of, but its visual appearance is worth the time donated to help it thrive. Grow in a location with stable temperatures and bright indirect to full sun away from air vents or drafts. Locating within a few feet from a southern or western facing window is ideal. Fiddle Leaf Fig prefers soil to be consistently and evenly moist with a brief drying out between waterings. To keep your plant healthy, feed it once a month with an organic slow-release fertilizer.

COMMON NAME: FISHBONE CACTUS, ZIG ZAG CACTUS
BOTANICAL NAME: DISOCACTUS ANGULIGER
LIGHTING REQUIREMENTS: BRIGHT INDIRECT
SOIL MOISTURE NEEDS: LOW, WELL DRAINED
PET FRIENDLY: YES

The Fishbone cactus displays long-jointed stems that resemble the bones of a fish. Growing to a mature size of two to three feet in diameter, Fishbone cactus prefers well-drained soil and a location with plenty of bright indirect light such as a west or east facing window. Water when the top couple of inches of soil are dry and avoid direct sunlight as it can scorch the leaves. To give the plant an extra boost of hydration, mist regularly. Fertilize once in spring and then again in summer to promote growth and blooms and prune to keep it in shape. In autumn, heavily scented blooms in shades of yellow, pink, or green come out after dark and live for one night on a mature plant and if the conditions are right. In the wild, and rarely indoors, this beauty grows an edible gooseberry-like fruit.

COMMON NAME: FISHBONE PRAYER PLANT
BOTANICAL NAME: CALATHEA BURLE-MARXII
LIGHTING REQUIREMENTS: BRIGHT INDIRECT
SOIL MOISTURE NEEDS: MEDIUM, WELL DRAINED
PET FRIENDLY: YES

Known for its attractive striped, herringbone-patterned leaves, Fishbone Prayer Plant prefers bright, indirect light, but it can tolerate lower light levels. Keep the soil consistently moist, but not wet and water when the top inch of soil is dry. This plant thrives in higher humidity, making it ideal for kitchens and bathrooms. Use a well-draining potting mix formulated for tropical plants and feed monthly during the growing season from spring through summer. Trim away any yellowing or damaged leaves to encourage healthy growth and clean the leaves to keep them dust free. Like other prayer plants, Fishbone Prayer Plant folds its leaves at night. If leaves appear droopy, the plant may need more humidity or more light. This plant reaches a mature size of two feet tall by wide.

COMMON NAME: FRIENDSHIP PLANT
BOTANICAL NAME: PILEA INVOLUCRATA
LIGHTING REQUIREMENTS: BRIGHT INDIRECT
SOIL MOISTURE NEEDS: MEDIUM, WELL DRAINED
PET FRIENDLY: YES

Friendship Plant is a low maintenance houseplant known for its textured, quilted leaves, ranging in appearance from deep green to bronze, with purple or reddish undersides. It stays relatively compact, usually growing to about 6-12 inches tall, making it suitable for tabletops or shelves. Pilea prefers bright indirect light, moderate humidity, and a slightly moist, well-draining soil. Clusters of small greenish-white blooms may appear when growing indoors, although rare. Pinch back stems to promote bushier growth and rotate the plant periodically to encourage even growth, as they tend to lean towards the light. During the growing season, feed with a balanced, diluted liquid fertilizer. Friendship Plant can easily be propagated by cuttings, making them perfect for sharing with friends.

COMMON NAME: JADE PLANT
BOTANICAL NAME: CRASSULA OVATA
LIGHTING REQUIREMENTS: HIGH
SOIL MOISTURE NEEDS: LOW, WELL DRAINED
PET FRIENDLY: NO

Jade Plant is a popular succulent known for its thick, oval-shaped leaves and sturdy, tree-like structure, growing up to three feet tall in optimal conditions. Grow in a well-draining succulent or cactus mix in full sun, such as a southern or western window and allow the soil to dry out in between waterings. Rotate the plant occasionally to promote even growth and wipe down leaves to improve light absorption. Watch for signs of Mealy Bug, especially in late fall to winter, and treat foliage with soapy water, alcohol, or insecticide. Feed a couple of times during the growing season with a balanced diluted fertilizer. If you have a mature Jade Plant, and it is in the perfect growing conditions, you may be rewarded with star-shaped white blooms during the fall or winter months.

COMMON NAME: JADE PLANT, GOLLUM JADE
BOTANICAL NAME: CRASSULA OVATA ET'S FINGERS
LIGHTING REQUIREMENTS: BRIGHT INDIRECT TO HIGH
SOIL MOISTURE NEEDS: LOW, WELL DRAINED
PET FRIENDLY: NO

Displaying elongated, tubular leaves, often with red tips resembling fingers, this unusual form of Jade is a popular choice among succulent lovers. Grow ET's Fingers in bright, indirect light to full sun. It can take some direct sun, such as a southern or western exposure, but monitor for fading, which could mean scorching of the leaves. As with other Jade, plant in a well-draining succulent or cactus mix and water sparingly. Feed with a balanced fertilizer at half strength every two to four weeks during the growing season. This cultivar can easily be propagated by stem or leaf cuttings. Allow cuttings to dry out for a day or two, then place in a well-draining soil with rooting medium. The same process applies to traditional Jade.

COMMON NAME: JADE PLANT, RIPPLE JADE
BOTANICAL NAME: CRASSULA ARBORESCENS UNDULATIFOLIA
LIGHTING REQUIREMENTS: BRIGHT INDIRECT TO HIGH
SOIL MOISTURE NEEDS: LOW, WELL DRAINED
PET FRIENDLY: NO

Ripple Jade is another perfect addition to your succulent collection exhibiting wavy, rippled leaves and growing to one to two feet tall indoors. Place in bright indirect to high light such as a southern or western exposure for at least four hours a day and plant in a well-draining succulent or cactus mix. Allow partial drying and water when the top couple of inches of soil feel dry. This cultivar may show scorching of the leaves if the plant is receiving too much direct sun or appear leggy in too little light and may need to be moved to a more optimum location. To keep your plant healthy, fertilize with a balanced plant food at half strength once a month during the growing season. Prune to shape as needed and repot every two to three years to maintain growth.

COMMON NAME: KALANCHOE
BOTANICAL NAME: KALANCHOE BLOSSFELDIANA
LIGHTING REQUIREMENTS: BRIGHT INDIRECT
SOIL MOISTURE NEEDS: MODERATE, WELL DRAINED
PET FRIENDLY: NO

Kalanchoe displays fleshy green leaves and clusters of orange, pink, yellow, red, or white blooms that can last for several weeks to months when cared for. It typically grows up to twelve to eighteen inches tall indoors, depending on the species and conditions. Grow Kalanchoe in bright, indirect sun in a well-draining succulent or cactus mix and water when the top inch of soil feels dry. Feed with a balanced fertilizer at half strength during the growing season. This succulent does go through a dormant period in late summer to early fall when it loses its leaves and produces new buds. To encourage Kalanchoe to rebloom, provide a period of darkness (about fourteen hours per night) for 6-8 weeks in fall to early winter. Trim off dead flowers and leggy growth to encourage fullness.

COMMON NAME: LADY PALM
BOTANICAL NAME: RHAPIS EXCELSA
LIGHTING REQUIREMENTS: BRIGHT INDIRECT
SOIL MOISTURE NEEDS: MODERATE, WELL DRAINED
PET FRIENDLY: YES

Exhibiting graceful, deep green fan-like leaves and multiple stems, Lady Palm is a welcomed addition to the home garden. Growing to approximately six feet high by four feet wide, Lady Palm prefers bright indirect light but can tolerate lower light conditions. Plant in a well-draining potting mix with perlite for aeration and feed monthly during the growing season with a balanced water-soluble fertilizer. As with other palms, this plant does prefer moderate to high humidity which can be achieved by misting or using a humidity tray. Repot every two to three years or when the plant becomes rootbound. The Lady Palm is generally low maintenance and good for beginners. Regular dusting of the leaves helps maintain its glossy appearance and supports its air purifying capabilities.

COMMON NAME: LIVING STONE
BOTANICAL NAME: LITHOPS
LIGHTING REQUIREMENTS: BRIGHT
SOIL MOISTURE NEEDS: LOW, WELL DRAINED
PET FRIENDLY: NO

Lithops, often called "living stones" are unique, stone-like succulents from the deserts of southern Africa. Each plant grows to an inch or two in height and consists of a pair of thick, fused leaves with a cleft in the middle. Colors vary in earth tones from gray to green, beige or brown and daisy-like flowers, typically white or yellow, emerge from the cleft between the leaves, usually in autumn. Lithops need bright, direct sunlight such as a sunny windowsill and a well-draining, gritty cactus or succulent mix with sand or perlite. Use a shallow pot and allow the soil to completely dry out in between watering and water sparingly, as they are very drought tolerant. Lithops prefer low humidity, and no fertilizer is really needed, but if desired, use a diluted low nitrogen cactus food in spring.

COMMON NAME: LUCKY BAMBOO
BOTANICAL NAME: DRACAENA SANDERIANA
LIGHTING REQUIREMENTS: BRIGHT INDIRECT
SOIL MOISTURE NEEDS: MODERATE
PET FRIENDLY: NO

Lucky Bamboo is an attractive and easy-care houseplant believed according to the principle of Feng Shui to foster positive energy, good luck, and prosperity and can be grown either in a well-drained potting soil or pebble tray with water. Provide bright indirect lighting such as a northern or eastern window or beneath a skylight and water using filtered or distilled water. Water when the top layer of soil is dry or if in a pebble tray add new filtered water every other week and feed with a weak liquid fertilizer every few months, a method which I have found to be ideal. Lucky Bamboo is exceptionally low maintenance. Yellowing of leaves or stems is an indication of overwatering, chemicals in the water, too much direct lighting or over fertilization. Leaves curling is a sign of lack of moisture.

COMMON NAME: MEZOO PLANT
BOTANICAL NAME: DOROTHEANTHUS BELLIDIFORMIS
LIGHTING REQUIREMENTS: BRIGHT INDIRECT
SOIL MOISTURE NEEDS: LOW
PET FRIENDLY: NO

The Mezoo Plant displays an attractive compact growth habit with tailing stems that can reach twelve to twenty-four inches in length. This makes it ideal for hanging baskets or as a cascading plant in pots. It produces small, daisy-like flowers around one inch across that have a vibrant pink, magenta or red color with a yellow center. To encourage frequent blooms indoors, place in a sunny spot with several hours of filtered light daily. Mezoo Plant prefers a well-draining cactus or succulent mix and a dry environment over damp soil. With its succulent like leaves, it is somewhat drought tolerant and will also tolerate low humidity. Feed with a balanced diluted fertilizer once a month during the growing season and trim back stems as needed to maintain shape and fullness.

COMMON NAME: MEXICAN SNOWBALL, HENS & CHICKS
BOTANICAL NAME: ECHEVERIA ELEGANS
LIGHTING REQUIREMENTS: BRIGHT
SOIL MOISTURE NEEDS: LOW, WELL DRAINED
PET FRIENDLY: YES

Echeveria, also known as Mexican Snowball or Hens & Chicks is an easy-care succulent displaying attractive foliage in a compact rounded habit. Rosettes can grow to a height and width of one to four inches tall by two to twelve inches in diameter (depending on the variety) and may produce tall stalks with insignificant orange blooms. Grow this succulent in a well-drained soil in a bright location with six or more hours of sunlight, as in a southern or western windowsill. Thoroughly soak the soil then allow it to dry out in between waterings to avoid root rot. If your plant is becoming leggy, it is a sign that it may require more sun. I also cut off the flower stalks after bloom to put energy back into the plant. It is normal for older plants to become top heavy and may simply need repotting.

COMMON NAME: MISTLETOE CACTUS
BOTANICAL NAME: RHIPSALIS BACCIFERA
LIGHTING REQUIREMENTS: BRIGHT
SOIL MOISTURE NEEDS: LOW TO MODERATE, WELL DRAINED
PET FRIENDLY: YES

This unique epiphytic cactus is native to rainforests, but unlike desert cacti it prefers more humidity and shade. With its low demands, Mistletoe Cactus makes an interesting and adaptable addition to your houseplant collection. Mistletoe Cactus prefers a loose potting mix like those used for orchids and succulents and moderate watering when the top inch of soil is dry. Reduce watering in winter, but do not allow the soil to dry out. Place in bright indirect light and avoid direct sun, as it can scorch the leaves. This plant thrives in average room temperature with higher humidity, which can be achieved with a humidifier in drier areas. Trim back stems as needed to control the plant's size and shape and feed monthly with a balanced, diluted cactus or orchid fertilizer.

COMMON NAME: MONEY TREE
BOTANICAL NAME: PACHIRA AQUATICA
LIGHTING REQUIREMENTS: BRIGHT INDIRECT
SOIL MOISTURE NEEDS: MODERATE
ADDITIONAL: PREFERS HIGH HUMIDITY
PET FRIENDLY: YES

In Feng Shui, the Money Tree is believed to bring luck, wealth, and prosperity. Growing to three to six feet indoors, position in bright, indirect light and water thoroughly when the top one to two inches of soil are dry. Money Tree prefers a soil with good drainage and higher humidity levels, which can be accomplished by misting the leaves occasionally or placing near a humidifier in drier locations. Prune back any leggy or yellowing growth and feed monthly with a balanced fertilizer during the growing season.

COMMON NAME: NERVE PLANT, MOSAIC PLANT
BOTANICAL NAME: FITTONIA ALBIVENIS 'BIG LEAF'
LIGHTING REQUIREMENTS: BRIGHT INDIRECT
SOIL MOISTURE NEEDS: HIGH
ADDITIONAL: PREFERS HIGH HUMIDITY
PET FRIENDLY: YES

Fittonia, or Nerve Plant is an attractive houseplant that lives up to its name with its constant need for moisture. Skip one watering and it will have the nerve to wilt like a drama queen until it gets its way! The name Nerve Plant really stems from what it is prized for, its deep green leaves that are networked with either pink, white, or red veins resembling the nervous system. Slow growing, Nerve Plant can reach a height of 3 to 6 inches tall with a trailing spread of 12 to 18 inches and prefers a location with bright indirect light away from draft. A soil high in peat moss, which is kept constantly moist, but well-drained is best. The ideal location for this beauty is in a northern or eastern windowsill or better yet in a kitchen or bathroom, where it will receive the humidity that it loves. Another option is to create a more humid environment by placing the pot on a tray filled with pebbles and water or growing it in a terrarium.

There are several varieties of Fittonia to choose from, ranging in leaf size and coloration depending on the cultivar. The two main categories are white Nerve plant displaying white or silvery veins, and red or pink Nerve Plant with red or pink veins. Although the plant rarely flowers in cultivation, with the right conditions it can produce insignificant blooms on reddish or yellowish-white spikes. A dwarf version, 'Mini Pink' (Figure 1) has smaller leaves and grows to just 3 to 12 inches tall.

FIGURE 1: FITTONIA ALBIVENIS 'MINI PINK'

Feed your Nerve Plant with a balanced 5-5-5 houseplant fertilizer diluted to half strength every four to six weeks during their growing season in spring and summer. If your plant becomes leggy, pinching off the longer growth will help to keep it full.

COMMON NAME: NEVER-NEVER PLANT
BOTANICAL NAME: CTENANTHE SETOSA 'GREY STAR'
LIGHTING REQUIREMENTS: BRIGHT INDIRECT
SOIL MOISTURE NEEDS: MODERATE
PET FRIENDLY: NO

Ctenanthe setosa, commonly known as Never-Never plant is a colorful tropical plant with bold patterned foliage that adds a decorative touch to your indoor space. Never-Never plant grows to a mature size of three feet tall by wide and prefers a location with warm temperatures, bright to medium indirect light, moderately moist soil, and medium humidity. Keep your plant out of direct sun as it can burn the leaves and water when the top layer of soil feels slightly dry to the touch. Curling leaves indicate improper watering. Yellow leaves are a sign of too much watering while brown crispy leaves indicate not enough moisture or humidity. Ctenanthe prefer filtered or distilled water and are not heavy feeders. Fertilize with a balanced plant food once a month during the growing season.

COMMON NAME: NORFOLK ISLAND PINE
BOTANICAL NAME: ARAUCARIA HETEROPHYLLA
LIGHTING REQUIREMENTS: BRIGHT INDIRECT
SOIL MOISTURE NEEDS: MODERATE
PET FRIENDLY: NO

Native to the Norfolk Island near Australia, this plant with its soft, feathery needles and graceful layered look has become a popular houseplant and is often seen being sold during the holiday season. Indoors, it can grow up to 5-8 feet tall and prefers bright indirect lighting and a lightly moist well-draining soil. These trees prefer slightly higher humidity, so misting occasionally or placing near a humidity tray is beneficial. During the growing season in spring and summer, feed every four to six weeks with a water-soluble fertilizer at half strength.

COMMON NAME: ORCHID. MOTH ORCHID, PHALAENOPSIS ORCHID
BOTANICAL NAME PHALAENOPSIS AMABILIS
LIGHTING REQUIREMENTS: BRIGHT INDIRECT
SOIL MOISTURE NEEDS: MODERATE, WELL DRAINED, PREFERS HIGH
HUMIDITY
PET FRIENDLY: YES

Growing Moth Orchid can be a rewarding experience as they are known for their long-lasting elegant blooms and relatively low maintenance needs. Plant in a bark-based or sphagnum moss medium and place in bright, indirect light such as an eastern or western facing window. If the leaves turn dark green, the plant may need more light, verses if yellowish, it may be getting too much light. Orchids like a balanced approach to watering. Water thoroughly, allowing the water to drain out, and the growing medium to dry slightly between waterings. Moth Orchids prefer higher humidity (50-70%). This can be achieved by placing a pebble tray under the pot or misting lightly around the plant. Fertilize with a balanced orchid fertilizer every two to four weeks during the growing season.

COMMON NAME: PARLOR PALM
BOTANICAL NAME: CHAMAEDOREA ELEGANS
LIGHTING REQUIREMENTS: MEDIUM/LOW
SOIL MOISTURE NEEDS: MODERATELY MOIST
PET FRIENDLY: YES

Parlor Palm is a popular low maintenance houseplant known for its lush green arching foliage, air cleansing qualities, pet-friendliness, and adaptability to low light conditions. While it reaches much larger sizes in its natural habitat, as a houseplant Parlor Palm grows to a height and width of approximately two to six feet tall by two to three feet wide with the proper conditions. Ideally, Parlor Plam prefers medium diffused light, but it can tolerate lower lighting conditions such as near a northern window. Plant in an organically rich, acidic to neutral pH all-purpose potting mix and keep the soil moderately moist, but not soggy. Trim off any fronds which have browned or yellowed at the base to maintain a full and healthy plant.

COMMON NAME: PEACE LILY
BOTANICAL NAME: SPATHIPHYLLUM
LIGHTING REQUIREMENTS: LOW TO BRIGHT INDIRECT
SOIL MOISTURE NEEDS: MOIST, WELL-DRAINED
PET FRIENDLY: NO

Peace Lily (Spathiphyllum) are known for their beautiful green foliage and white or creamy colored spathes that are produced often in springtime and again in fall under the right conditions. This plant is associated with peace, purity, and healing, making them popular choices for indoor growing as well as gifts. Grow in low to bright indirect light, such as near an eastern or northern window and keep the soil consistently moist, but not wet. Water thoroughly when the top inch of soil feels dry (typically once a week), ensure good drainage and avoid letting the pot sit in water. The plant will wilt slightly when in need of moisture. Peace Lily prefer slightly higher humidity and are light feeders. Feed every 6-8 weeks during the growing season. Trim off any yellow or browning leaves to preserve health.

COMMON NAME: PEACOCK PLANT
BOTANICAL NAME: CALATHEA MAKOYANA
LIGHTING REQUIREMENTS: MEDIUM, DIFFUSED, INDIRECT LIGHT
SOIL MOISTURE NEEDS: MODERATELY MOIST, PREFERS HIGH HUMIDITY
PET FRIENDLY: YES

Peacock Plant (Calathea makoyana) is widely known for its outstanding foliage displaying an array of color. Calathea prefer a location with medium to diffused light, a moderately moist soil, and ideally a humidity level of sixty percent or higher. Grouping plants together or using a pebble tray can help achieve this goal. Calathea stays compact at a height and width of 1-2 feet tall by wide and are known to constantly push out new buds and foliage. Remove any faded or browned leaves to keep your plant healthy. From experience, growing this plant beneath a skylight, while watering it once a week is ideal. There are several varieties to choose from, each with a beautiful display of striking foliage including Calathea makoyana 'Medallion', 'Green Beauty' or 'Dottie' with pinkish highlights.

COMMON NAME: PEPEROMIA
BOTANICAL NAME: PEPEROMIA CAPERATA
LIGHTING REQUIREMENTS: MEDIUM, DIFFUSED, INDIRECT LIGHT
SOIL MOISTURE NEEDS: MODERATELY MOIST
PET FRIENDLY: YES

Peperomia is an attractive houseplant with heart-shaped leaves displaying heavy ridging and crinkling which gives them an interesting look. Peperomia prefer a brightly lit area such as an eastern facing window, medium to high humidity and a well-drained potting mix containing coco coir and perlite for good aeration. Keep your plant moderately watered but allow the top layer of soil to dry slightly to the touch. To keep your plant robust, pinch back leggy growth and feed it with an all-purpose plant food during the growing season. Peperomia do not have large root systems, grow slowly to 1-2 feet and do best when grown in small containers. There are several varieties of Peperomia to choose from including newer varieties displaying light green, smooth or pointed leaves with red undersides.

COMMON NAME: PHILODENDRON GOLDEN CROCODILE
BOTANICAL NAME: PHILODENDRON PINNATIFIDUM 'MELINONII'
LIGHTING REQUIREMENTS: MEDIUM, BRIGHT INDIRECT
SOIL MOISTURE NEEDS: MODERATELY MOIST, WELL-DRAINED
PET FRIENDLY: NO

Philodendron Golden Crocodile features eye-catching golden-yellow leaves with orange-tinged new growth that will quickly win your heart. With maturity the foliage will develop tooth-like serrations and leaves can reach more than two feet long. Give this cultivar medium to bright indirect lighting such as within three to four feet of an eastern or western windowsill or position under grow lights. Direct morning sun followed by dappled afternoon shade is ideal. This plant prefers average room temperature, normal to slightly higher humidity, and a well-drained soil containing perlite. Keep the soil moderately moist, but not wet. It is important to allow the top half or so of potting mix to dry in between waterings. Feed with a well-balanced fertilizer monthly during the growing season.

COMMON NAME: PHILODENDRON MOONLIGHT
BOTANICAL NAME: PHILODENDRON HEDERACEUM 'MOONLIGHT'
LIGHTING REQUIREMENTS: MEDIUM, BRIGHT INDIRECT
SOIL MOISTURE NEEDS: MODERATELY MOIST
PET FRIENDLY: NO

Known for its large striking chartreuse to lime-green leaves on a bushy compact plant, Philodendron Moonlight makes an eye-catching addition to indoor spaces. Position in bright, indirect light, such as an eastern facing window or several feet from a western window, and keep the soil consistently moist, but not wet. Water when the top inch of soil feels dry and reduce watering in winter. Feed this plant with a balanced water-soluble fertilizer every four to six weeks during spring and summer and reduce or stop feeding in winter. Philodendron thrives in moderate to high humidity, which can be achieved by placing around other plants, use of a humidifier, pebble tray or misting. Keep in a warm environment, ideally between 65-80 degrees F (18-27 C) and protect it from cold drafts.

COMMON NAME: PHILODENDRON WINTERBOURN
BOTANICAL NAME: PHILODENDRON 'XANADU' DWARF FORM
LIGHTING REQUIREMENTS: MEDIUM, BRIGHT INDIRECT
SOIL MOISTURE NEEDS: MODERATELY MOIST
PET FRIENDLY: NO

Philodendron Winterbourn, commonly known as 'Xanadu', is a beautiful, compact philodendron variety with deeply lobed glossy green leaves that give it a lush, tropical look. Indoors, it grows to a manageable size, reaching around two to four feet tall and wide, making it suitable for smaller spaces. Grow in bright, indirect light in a well-draining potting mix containing organic matter such as perlite or orchid bark to improve aeration. Water when the top inch of soil feels dry but be cautious not to overwater, as 'Xanadu' is sensitive to soggy soil, which would be indicated by yellowing leaves. As with other philodendron, feed 'Xanadu' every four to six weeks during the growing season with a balanced liquid fertilizer and reduce watering in winter as the plant's growth slows.

COMMON NAME: PHILODENDRON IMPERIAL GREEN
BOTANICAL NAME: PHILODENDRON ERUBESCENS 'IMPERIAL GREEN'
LIGHTING REQUIREMENTS: MEDIUM, BRIGHT INDIRECT
SOIL MOISTURE NEEDS: MODERATELY MOIST
PET FRIENDLY: NO

A striking low maintenance variety of philodendron, 'Imperial Queen' displays broad, oval-shaped glossy green leaves with burgundy edges becoming greener as they mature. This cultivar displays a compact, upright growth habit and robust thick foliage, growing to a height of two to three feet indoors. Plant in a well-draining potting mix containing perlite or orchid bark and place in bright, indirect to medium light. Avoid placing in direct light to prevent leaf scorch. Water when the top inch of soil feels dry and keep consistently moist, but never wet. As with other philodendron, 'Imperial Queen' prefers moderate to high humidity and feeding with a balanced liquid fertilizer during the growing months. It can be propagated by stem cuttings containing at least one node in either soil or water.

COMMON NAME: PHILODENDRON IMPERIAL RED
BOTANICAL NAME: PHILODENDRON ERUBESCENS 'IMPERIAL RED'
LIGHTING REQUIREMENTS: MEDIUM, BRIGHT INDIRECT
SOIL MOISTURE NEEDS: MODERATELY MOIST
PET FRIENDLY: NO

With striking glossy, reddish orange leaves that transition to dark green as they mature, Philodendron 'Imperial Red' displays a compact growth habit, reaching two to three feet in height indoors, making it suitable for tabletop or floor displays. 'Imperial Red' prefers bright, indirect light but can adapt to medium light and thrives in moderate to high humidity. Use a well-draining potting mix with perlite to help with aeration and drainage and water when the top inch of soil feels dry. Be careful not to overwater, as this plant does not tolerate soggy soil, and feed monthly with a balanced liquid fertilizer during the growing season. Philodendron do not like to be rootbound. Repot if plant growth diminishes, water drains too quickly or if the plant is showing signs of wilting or yellowing leaves.

COMMON NAME: PINK LADY OR PINK PANTHER
BOTANICAL NAME: CALLISIA REPENS 'PINK PANTHER'
LIGHTING REQUIREMENTS: BRIGHT FULL SUN
SOIL MOISTURE NEEDS: MODERATELY MOIST
PET FRIENDLY: NO

The Pink Lady Callisia is a compact, trailing plant known for its attractive variegated leaves in shades of green, pink, and purple. It typically grows up to four to six inches in height and spreads as it trails, making it ideal for hanging baskets or tabletop planters. Position Pink Lady in bright, indirect sunlight. Note: Some direct morning light can help to enhance its pink hues. Use a well-draining potting mix, such as one formulated for succulents or cacti to prevent excess water around the roots and water when the top inch of soil feels dry. Regular trimming will help to keep the plant bushy and prevent it from becoming too leggy. Feed every four to six weeks during the growing season to keep your plant at its best. Small white flowers may appear among the leaves during spring.

COMMON NAME: POINSETTIA, CHRISTMAS STAR
BOTANICAL NAME: EUPHORBIA PULCHERRIMA
LIGHTING REQUIREMENTS: BRIGHT INDIRECT
SOIL MOISTURE NEEDS: MODERATELY MOIST
PET FRIENDLY: NO, MILDLY TOXIC TO PETS. MILD IRRITATION

Poinsettia is a popular houseplant, especially around the holiday season, known for its bright colorful bracts, which are often mistaken for flowers. These bracts come in shades of red, pink, white and variegated varieties with small yellow flowers in the center, creating a festive appearance. Plant poinsettia in a well-draining potting mix and keep the soil consistently moist, but not wet. Water when the top inch of soil feels dry. Feed monthly with a balanced water-soluble fertilizer during the growing season and avoid fertilizing when in bloom. To get poinsettia to bloom the following year, reduce watering after the bracts fade and let it rest in a cool, dark place. Around October, provide with fourteen hours of darkness daily for 8-10 weeks to encourage bract color for the holiday season.

COMMON NAME: POLKA DOT PLANT (PINK)
BOTANICAL NAME: HYPOESTES PHYLLOSTACHYA
LIGHTING REQUIREMENTS: BRIGHT FILTERED
SOIL MOISTURE NEEDS: MODERATELY MOIST
PET FRIENDLY: YES

The Polka Dot Plant gets its name from its speckled leaves, which can come in shades of pink, red, green, and white, adding a pop of color to indoor spaces. Plant in a well-draining potting mix with organic matter and place in bright, indirect light. Too much direct sun can fade the colors on the leaves, while too little light can make the plant leggy. Water when the top inch of soil feels dry and keep the moisture consistent. This plant grows to a compact size of one to two feet tall at maturity and thrives in high humidity and warm temperatures. Avoid sudden changes as Polka Dot Plant is sensitive. Prune your plant regularly to encourage bushier growth and pinch off tips to maintain its compact shape. Feed with a balanced water-soluble fertilizer during the spring and summer.

COMMON NAME: POLKA DOT PLANT (WHITE)
BOTANICAL NAME: HYPOESTES PHYLLOSTACHYA 'SPLASH'
LIGHTING REQUIREMENTS: BRIGHT FILTERED
SOIL MOISTURE NEEDS: MODERATELY MOIST
PET FRIENDLY: YES

This variety of Polka Dot Plant is known for its striking leaves with white spots or speckles against a green background, giving it a unique appearance as if it had been splattered with paint. Having the same requirements as other Polka Dot Plants, plant in an organic soil containing peat moss or coconut coir and keep the soil consistently moist, but not wet. Feed monthly with a balanced fertilizer during the growing season. Polka Dot Plant may produce tiny, tubular flowers at the tips of the stems that range in color from lavender to light purple or pink. Unfortunately, these flowers may signal the end of the plant's life cycle, as they are short-lived, often lasting only one to two years. Polka Dot Plant is relatively easy to propagate through healthy stem cuttings either in soil or water.

COMMON NAME: PONYTAIL PALM
BOTANICAL NAME: BEAUCARNEA RECURVATA
LIGHTING REQUIREMENTS: BRIGHT INDIRECT LIGHT
SOIL MOISTURE NEEDS: LOW TO MODERATE, WELL-DRAINED
PET FRIENDLY: YES

Ponytail Palm is a distinctive houseplant known for its bulbous truck that stores water and its long, slender leaves that cascade downward, giving it a palm-like appearance. Despite its name, it is a succulent rather than a true palm. Growing to a height of 3 to 4 feet indoors, Ponytail Palm prefers bright indirect light as near a sunny window but can adapt to lower light, although growth may be slowed. Use a well-draining potting mix and ensure the pot has drainage holes. Water sparingly, allowing the soil to dry out in between watering and feed with a balanced, diluted fertilizer once a month during the growing season. Ponytail Palm prefers being slightly root-bound, so repotting is only needed every few years. It tolerates low humidity levels, making it ideal for most indoor environments.

COMMON NAME: POTHOS
BOTANICAL NAME: EPIPREMNUM AUREUM
LIGHTING REQUIREMENTS: BRIGHT, INDIRECT
SOIL MOISTURE NEEDS: MODERATELY MOIST, WELL-DRAINED
PET FRIENDLY: NO, EXTREMELY TOXIC

A popular low maintenance houseplant, Pothos is known for its trailing habit and heart-shaped leaves, often with variegation in shades of green, yellow, or white. This resilient plant thrives in a variety of indoor conditions, and tolerates some neglect, making it ideal for beginners. Pothos thrives in bright, indirect light but can tolerate lower light; however, some varieties may lose variegation. Allow the soil to dry out partially between waterings and feed every one to two months during the growing season. Prune back vines to control length and encourage bushier growth. Pruning just above a leaf node will encourage the plant to branch out. Pothos can be easily propagated by cutting a vine just below a node and placing it in moist soil or water until it roots.

COMMON NAME: POTHOS
BOTANICAL NAME: EPIPREMNUM AUREUM 'PEARLS & JADE'
LIGHTING REQUIREMENTS: BRIGHT, INDIRECT
SOIL MOISTURE NEEDS: MODERATELY MOIST, WELL-DRAINED
PET FRIENDLY: NO, EXTREMELY TOXIC

Pothos 'Pearls and Jade' has smaller leaves compared to other Pothos varieties and exhibits striking variegation along the edges of its foliage with green in the center and marbled with splashes of white and gray. While it can trail like other Pothos, it grows more slowly and compactly due to its variegation, which reduces chlorophyll production. 'Pearls and Jade' thrives in bright indirect light and the top inch of soil should be allowed to dry before watering. Use a well-draining potting mix with perlite or sand added for extra drainage. As with other Pothos, fertilize every one to two months with a balanced diluted fertilizer during the growing season (spring and summer) and prune as needed to control leggy growth. 'Pearls and Jade' can also be easily propagated by stem cuttings.

COMMON NAME: PRAYER PLANT
BOTANICAL NAME: MARANTA LEUCONEURA
LIGHTING REQUIREMENTS: MEDIUM, DIFFUSED
SOIL MOISTURE NEEDS: MODERATELY MOIST
PET FRIENDLY: YES
ADDITIONAL: PREFERS HIGH HUMIDITY

Prayer Plant (Maranta leuconeura) is one of the most beautiful houseplants for its interesting multi-colored foliage. While not the easiest plant to grow, finding the right location is key. Prayer Plant prefers a warm spot with bright diffused lighting such as near an east facing window or beneath a skylight, while keeping the soil moist, but not wet. Since Maranta can be sensitive to the fluoride in tap water, use filtered water or allow the water to sit. If the edges of leaves dry up more quickly in winter due to lack of humidity, placing a pebble tray beneath the plant can help. Marantha can grow to eighteen inches tall by twenty-four inches wide and its leaves move upward at night, resembling praying hands, hence the name. This process is a response to light and allows the plant to conserve moisture.

COMMON NAME: PURPLE HEART, PURPLE QUEEN
BOTANICAL NAME: TRADESCANTIA PALLIDA 'PURPLE HEART'
LIGHTING REQUIREMENTS: BRIGHT
SOIL MOISTURE NEEDS: MODERATELY MOIST
PET FRIENDLY: NO

Tradescantia 'Purple Heart', also known as 'Purple Queen', is a striking plant known for its trailing purple stems, attractive violet leaves and small pink or lavender blooms that appear at the leaf nodes during the warmer months. Its growth habit makes it ideal for hanging baskets. Use a well-draining potting mix and water when the top inch of soil feels dry. Tradescantia prefers bright, indirect light to maintain its vibrant purple color, though it can tolerate partial shade. Direct sunlight for a few hours can enhance color, but too much sun can scorch the leaves. Average home humidity levels are usually sufficient, though a slightly more humid environment can promote lush growth. Prune back leggy growth to encourage fullness and feed monthly during the growing season.

COMMON NAME: RATTLESNAKE PLANT
BOTANICAL NAME: GOEPPERTIA INSIGNIS
LIGHTING REQUIREMENTS: MEDIUM/DIFFUSED
SOIL MOISTURE NEEDS: MODERATELY MOIST
PET FRIENDLY: YES

'Rattlesnake Plant' is admired for its unique, wavy-edged leaves with rich purple undersides and dark outer green markings that resemble a rattlesnake's scales. As a member of the prayer plant family, it exhibits a bushy compact habit, reaching a height of one to two feet and prefers bright, indirect light as from an eastern window or a few feet from a western window, but tolerates lower light conditions. Direct sun can scorch its leaves causing brown spots. Plant in a well-draining potting mix and keep the soil consistently moist, but not wet. Filtered or distilled water is preferred, as tap water can cause sensitivity. 'Rattlesnake Plant' requires higher humidity to thrive and benefits from a humidifier or being grouped with other plants. Fertilize every four to six weeks during the growing season.

COMMON NAME: RUBBER PLANT
BOTANICAL NAME: FICUS ELASTICA 'MELANY'
LIGHTING REQUIREMENTS: BRIGHT INDIRECT
SOIL MOISTURE NEEDS: MODERATELY MOIST
PET FRIENDLY: NO

Displaying glossy oval shaped leaves ranging in size from five to over twelve inches in length, Rubber Plant is as popular today as it was back in the 1950's and has come a long way with several new cultivars. This newer cultivar displays deeper green leaves with a touch of burgundy. Ficus adapt well to indoor environments and require minimal care if they are placed in a location with plenty of bright light and consistent moisture. Position Rubber Plant in an eastern or western facing window or set back from a southern facing window and use a well-drained potting mix containing perlite to improve drainage and aeration. Keep the soil moderately moist, allowing the top 2-3 inches to dry in between and fertilize once a month at half strength during the growing season to keep your plant healthy.

107

COMMON NAME: RUBBER PLANT (VARIEGATED)
BOTANICAL NAME: FICUS ELASTICA 'TINEKE'
LIGHTING REQUIREMENTS: BRIGHT INDIRECT
SOIL MOISTURE NEEDS: MODERATELY MOIST
PET FRIENDLY: NO

Ficus elastica 'Tineke' is one of the most popular and easy to grow species of Rubber Plant displaying striking reddish-pink tones bordering green and cream foliage while the new growth appears deep burgundy red. This cultivar grows to a height of two to ten feet tall by one to two feet wide and prefers a location with bright indirect light away from direct sun. Water when the top layer of soil is dry to the touch. As with other members of the Ficus family, avoid areas with drafts and feed with a half strength fertilizer during the growing months. Ficus do benefit from occasional tidying to encourage development of new healthy foliage. Trim off any unhealthy leaves or leggy stems to improve appearance. Rubber Plant can be propagated from stem cuttings in spring using a rooting hormone in soil.

COMMON NAME: RUBBER PLANT, FICUS MOONSHINE
BOTANICAL NAME: FICUS ELASTICA 'SHIVEREANA'
LIGHTING REQUIREMENTS: BRIGHT INDIRECT
SOIL MOISTURE NEEDS: MODERATELY MOIST
PET FRIENDLY: NO

A unique and less common variety of Rubber Plant is Ficus elastica 'Shivereana', commonly referred to as 'Moonshine' due to its unusual moonlight appearance. Ficus elastica 'Shivereana' displays variegated lime green foliage dotted with specks of cream, white and darker green and can develop peachy tones depending on lighting. While this cultivar can be more sensitive to being moved when compared to other Rubber plants, the care for this cultivar is the same and rotating your plant often will maintain its variegation. 'Shivereana' is slower growing but can reach up to six feet indoors. Helpful Tip: Most Ficus prefer to be rootbound but will need to be repotted when the roots are growing out of the bottom of the pot. Loosen roots slightly and repot into a pot that is one size larger adding fresh soil.

COMMON NAME: SAGO PALM
BOTANICAL NAME: CYCAS REVOLUTA
LIGHTING REQUIREMENTS: BRIGHT
SOIL MOISTURE NEEDS: LOW
PET FRIENDLY: NO, EXTREMELY TOXIC

Sago Palm is a member of the cycad family and one of the most ancient of plant species, dating to the Mesozoic Era, some 66-252 million years ago. Introduced to Europe and North America by traveling explorers and botanists in the 18th and 19th centuries, Sago Palm displays stiff, feather-like leaves emerging from a thick rugged trunk and grows to two to three feet in height indoors. Although it is not a true palm, it has a similar appearance, giving it a tropical look. Grow Sago Palm in bright light in a well-draining soil mix and water sparingly, allowing the top inch of soil to dry out between. They are sensitive to overwatering, which can cause root rot. Prune any yellow or dead fronds near the base and fertilize every two to three months during the growing season. Avoid around pets.

COMMON NAME: SILVER TREE PLANT
BOTANICAL NAME: PILEA SPRUCEANA
LIGHTING REQUIREMENTS: BRIGHT INDIRECT
SOIL MOISTURE NEEDS: MODERATE
PET FRIENDLY: YES

Popular for its uniquely patterned foliage, 'Silver Tree', often referred to 'Silver Plant', displays crinkly leaves with a striking metallic silver pattern on a deep green or bronze background. It is a mounding houseplant that typically grows to six to twelve inches tall and wide, making it ideal for smaller spaces. Locate in bright, indirect light to keep its silver coloring and water when the top inch of soil feels dry, keeping the soil consistently moist, but not wet. Pilea prefers higher humidity so consider placing it in a humid room such as a bathroom or kitchen and plant in a well-draining peat-based potting mix. Fertilize once a month during spring and summer and prune lightly if necessary to maintain shape and encourage fullness. With the right balance of light, humidity and moisture, this plant can thrive indoors.

COMMON NAME: SNAKE PLANT (DWARF)
BOTANICAL NAME: SANSEVIERIA TRIFASCIATA 'FUTURA SUPERBA'
LIGHTING: LOW
SOIL MOISTURE NEEDS: LOW
PER FRIENDLY: NO

Snake Plant 'Futura Superba' is a dwarf species of Sansevieria with shorter and broader swordlike leaves, often with dark coloring and light green horizontal variegation. The leaves are outlined with narrow creamy-yellow edges, giving the plant a bold sculptural look. It grows to a height of approximately twelve to eighteen inches, which is more compact than other varieties of Snake Plant, making it ideal for smaller spaces, such as kitchen windowsills and bathroom counters. Snake Plants are adaptable and can tolerate low lighting, but grow best in bright, indirect light. Water sparingly, as they are drought tolerant and prone to root rot if overwatered. 'Futura Superba' will thrive in average indoor humidity and are adaptable to both dry and slightly humid conditions.

112

COMMON NAME: SNAKE PLANT
BOTANICAL NAME: SANSEVIERIA TRIFASCIATA 'LAURENTII'
LIGHTING: LOW
SOIL MOISTURE NEEDS: LOW
PET FRIENDLY: NO

Snake Plant 'Trifasciata Laurentii' is known for its long sword-shaped leaves with green bands and yellow edges, that can reach a height of two to four feet, with new shoots emerging from the base and forming a dense clump. It has the same requirements as 'Futura Superba', making it ideal for just about any home setting. Snake Plants are light feeders. Feed monthly during the growing season with a balanced liquid plant food at half strength. They are also known for their beneficial air purifying properties, removing toxins like formaldehyde and benzene from the indoor air.

COMMON NAME: SNAKE PLANT CYLINDRICAL
BOTANICAL NAME: SANSEVIERIA CYLINDRICA
LIGHTING: BRIGHT, INDIRECT
SOIL MOISTURE NEEDS: LOW
PET FRIENDLY: NO

The Cylindrical Snake Plant is a unique variety of Sansevieria characterized by its round dark green tube-like leaves with gray-green stripes that can reach three feet tall. Leaves typically grow in a fan shape and can be braided or curved for a decorative effect. Cylindrical Snake Plants are highly adaptive and can tolerate low light but do best in bright indirect light to encourage faster growth. The plant does well in average indoor humidity and is drought tolerant, so water sparingly. Plant in a well-draining, sandy potting soil such as a cacti or succulent mix to ensure proper drainage. Feed with a balanced fertilizer at half strength during the growing season. Like other Snake Plants, this variety is also an excellent air purifier, and its easy care makes it a great choice for beginners.

COMMON NAME: SONG OF JAMAICA
BOTANICAL NAME: DRACAENA REFLEXA
LIGHTING: BRIGHT DIFFUSED
SOIL MOISTURE NEEDS: MODERATE, WELL-DRAINED
ADDITIONAL: PREFERS HIGH HUMIDITY
PET FRIENDLY: NO

Song of Jamaica displays narrow, bright green lance-shaped leaves with yellow stripes, and grows up to 3 to 6 feet indoors. It prefers bright, indirect light but can tolerate lower light levels. Song of Jamaica thrives in moderate to high humidity, which can be accomplished by misting the leaves occasionally, placing in a pebble tray or grouping with other plants. Plant in a well-draining potting mix and feed it with a balanced liquid fertilizer every four to six weeks during spring and summer and water when the top one to two inches of soil feel dry. To maintain a healthy plant, prune off any yellow or dead leaves and repot it every 2 to 3 years when the plant outgrows its container. Song of Jamaica is known to be air purifying.

COMMON NAME: SPIDER PLANT
BOTANICAL NAME: CHLOROPHYTUM COMOSUM
LIGHTING REQUIREMENTS: BRIGHT, INDIRECT
SOIL MOISTURE NEEDS: MODERATELY MOIST, WELL-DRAINED
PET FRIENDLY: YES

Air purifying and pet friendly, Spider Plant has long arching
variegated leaves that grow in rosettes. Grow in bright indirect
light in a well-draining soil and water when the top inch of soil is
dry. Remove any yellow or brown leaves and fertilize every 4-6
weeks during the growing season. Mature plants produce small
white flowers and offshoots that can be easily propagated to
create new plants. This low maintenance and resilient plant is
excellent for beginners and is perfect for shelves or hanging
planters.

COMMON NAME: SPLIT LEAF PHILODENDRON
BOTANICAL NAME: PHILODENDRON SELLOUM
LIGHTING REQUIREMENTS: BRIGHT, INDIRECT
SOIL MOISTURE NEEDS: MODERATELY MOIST, WELL-DRAINED
ADDITIONAL: PREFERS HIGH HUMIDITY
PET FRIENDLY: NO

Philodendron Selloum, also referred to as Spit Leaf or Lace Tree Philodendron, displays large deeply lobed green leaves that can grow to three feet long indoors. This upright growing philodendron prefers bright indirect light and a rich potting mix with perlite or orchid bark for increased drainage. The plant can reach an eventual five to six feet tall indoors with the optimum conditions and may develop aerial roots which can be left as is or tucked into the soil for support. To keep your plant healthy, wipe down the leaves periodically to remove dust and feed with a balanced liquid fertilizer every four to six weeks during the growing season. Philodendron thrives in higher humidity but can adapt to average conditions.

COMMON NAME: STAGHORN FERN
BOTANICAL NAME: PLATYCERIUM
LIGHTING REQUIREMENTS: BRIGHT, INDIRECT
SOIL MOISTURE NEEDS: CONSISTENT MOISTURE
ADDITIONAL: PREFERS HIGH HUMIDITY
PET FRIENDLY: YES

Adding a touch of the tropics with antler-shaped fronds and silvery green leaves with a slightly fuzzy texture, Staghorn Fern is an epiphyte preferring higher humidity (50-75%) which can be achieved with a using a humidifier, misting, or by placing in a bathroom or kitchen. Grow in bright, indirect light and plant in a well-draining potting mix containing orchid bark, perlite, or cactus soil. It can also be grown on wood or cork mounts with sphagnum moss. Soak the entire root ball in water when dry and allow it to drain. Feed with a diluted fertilizer once a month during spring and summer. Remove dead or damaged fronds, but do not remove the brown basal fronds, which are responsible for collecting water and nutrients for the plant.

COMMON NAME: STRING OF PEARLS
BOTANICAL NAME: SENECIO ROWLEYANUS
LIGHTING REQUIREMENTS: BRIGHT INDIRECT, DIFFUSED AFTERNOON SUN
SOIL MOISTURE NEEDS: LOW
PET FRIENDLY: NO

String of Pearls lives up to its name with small, spherical leaves resembling green pearls, growing along trailing stems that can grow two to three feet long indoors. Small white daisy-like flowers with a sweet cinnamon-like fragrance may appear during the summer under optimum conditions. Excellent for hanging baskets, this trailing succulent prefers warm home temperatures, a well-draining cactus or succulent mix and bright indirect light, protected from harsh afternoon rays. Water sparingly only when the soil is dry and apply a balanced all-purpose mix fertilizer diluted to half strength every four to six weeks during the growing season. String of Pearls can be easily propagated by stem cuttings. Lay the cuttings on the soil with the nodes touching or plant them slightly into moist soil.

COMMON NAME: STRING OF TEARS
BOTANICAL NAME: CURIO HERREANUS
LIGHTING REQUIREMENTS: BRIGHT INDIRECT, DIFFUSED AFTERNOON SUN
SOIL MOISTURE NEEDS: LOW
PET FRIENDLY: NO

String of Tears displays small, teardrop-shaped leaves that grow along trailing stems. Like String of Pearls, it is ideal for hanging planters where the stems can cascade. Plant in a well-draining cactus or succulent mix containing perlite or course sand to ensure proper drainage and locate in bright, indirect light such as an eastern window or a few feet from a western window. As with other succulents, water when the top layer of soil is dry and water sparingly. This plant is naturally adapted to arid environments and does not like to sit in water. Trim off any leggy or dead stems to promote fuller growth and feed during the growing season with a diluted balanced fertilizer at half strength. In optimum conditions, sweetly fragrant daisy-like white blooms may appear during the growing season.

COMMON NAME: STRING OF WATERMELONS
BOTANICAL NAME: CURIO HERREANUS 'WATERMELON'
LIGHTING REQUIREMENTS: BRIGHT INDIRECT, DIFFUSED AFTERNOON SUN
SOIL MOISTURE NEEDS: LOW
PET FRIENDLY: NO

Displaying oval-shaped leaves and striped patterns resembling watermelon rinds, String of Watermelons lives up to its name. Having the same growing requirements as String of Pearls and String of Tears, this easy-care succulent is perfect for beginner plant owners, as it thrives on infrequent watering and bright indirect light, while requiring a minimal amount of attention to keep it healthy. Grow String of Watermelons in average home temperatures and humidity. Like its predecessors, small white daisy-like flowers with a sweet cinnamon-like fragrance can add an extra touch. Hint: Slightly cooler temperatures in winter can help to promote blooms. Rotate the plant occasionally to maintain even growth, prune extra-long stems if the plant gets leggy and use the trimmings to propagate new plants!

121

COMMON NAME: SWISS CHEESE PLANT
BOTANICAL NAME: MONSTERA DELICIOSA
LIGHTING REQUIREMENTS: BRIGHT TO MEDIUM FILTERED, INDIRECT
SOIL MOISTURE NEEDS: SLIGHTLY MOIST, WELL-DRAINED
ADDITIONAL: PREFERS HIGH HUMIDITY
PET FRIENDLY: NO

Monstera are known for their natural leaf-holes, hence giving rise to their nickname, Swiss Cheese Plant. These openings are known as fenestrations and are believed to maximize sunlight reaching the plant by increasing surface area of the leaves. Quickly growing to 3-15 feet tall by 3-8 feet wide, Monstera are best grown in a well-drained potting mix and located in bright to medium indirect light. Monstera do not take well to salt buildup, so the use of filtered water every one to two weeks is best, while allowing the soil to slightly dry out in between. Keep Monstera out of direct sun and provide higher humidity by grouping with other plantings, use of a humidifier or pebble tray partially filled with water to achieve this effect.

122

COMMON NAME: SWISS CHEESE PLANT VARIEGATED (RARE SPECIES)
BOTANICAL NAME: MONSTERA DELICIOSA 'THAI CONSTELLATION'
LIGHTING REQUIREMENTS: BRIGHT TO MEDIUM FILTERED, INDIRECT
SOIL MOISTURE NEEDS: SLIGHTLY MOIST, WELL-DRAINED
ADDITIONAL: PREFERS HIGH HUMIDITY
PET FRIENDLY: NO

This extremely rare and beautiful hybrid of Monstera was formed by a genetic mutation and first discovered in Thailand. Its distinctive variegation, including bright white or cream splotches on dark green leaves along with large fenestrations as it matures makes this an outstanding piece. Monstera 'Thai Constellation' can slowly reach a mature size of up to 10-15 feet tall by 4-8 foot wide indoors with the right conditions. Provide bright to medium indirect lighting and a loamy moist, but well-drained soil, while allowing the top layer of soil to dry slightly in between waterings. Due to lack of availability and difficulty in propagation, this hybrid is costly, but if you are fortunate enough to encounter it, it could become a unique piece in your collection!

COMMON NAME: SWISS CHEESE PLANT (LITTLE SWISS MONSTERA)
BOTANICAL NAME: MONSTERA ADANSONII
LIGHTING REQUIREMENTS: BRIGHT TO MEDIUM FILTERED, INDIRECT
SOIL MOISTURE NEEDS: SLIGHTLY MOIST, WELL-DRAINED
ADDITIONAL: PREFERS HIGH HUMIDITY
PET FRIENDLY: NO

Monstera adansonii can be distinguished from M. deliciosa by having elongated leaves with fenestrations that are completely enclosed, thus resembling Swiss Cheese. Its trailing or climbing habit makes it ideal for hanging baskets, moss poles or trellises. Swiss Cheese Plant can grow to two to four feet tall indoors, prefers bight, indirect light, and a peat-based potting mix with good drainage. Use filtered or distilled water if your tap water is high in chlorine or salts and keep the soil consistently moist, but not wet. This attractive plant prefers higher humidity and should be protected from sudden temperature changes. Apply a balanced fertilizer at half strength monthly and trim leggy or damaged leaves to promote healthy growth.

COMMON NAME: THANKSGIVING CACTUS
BOTANICAL NAME: SCHLUMBERGERA TRUNCATA
LIGHTING REQUIREMENTS: BRIGHT LIGHT
SOIL MOISTURE NEEDS: LOW
PET FRIENDLY: YES

There are three species of this popular succulent, depending on bloom time. The most common variety, Thanksgiving cactus (Schlumbergera truncata) has very pointed, claw-shaped projections on the edges of each leaf, while Christmas cactus (Schlumbergera bridgesii) has more scalloped, or tear-drop shaped leaves and Easter cactus (Rhipsalidopsis gaertneri) has more rounded, smooth leaves. The ideal location for this plant is in a southern or western windowsill, where changing fall temperatures trigger blooming. Water every 2-3 weeks when the top third of the soil is dry and remove faded flowers to encourage more blooms. As new growth appears in spring, apply a weak strength fertilizer every 2-3 weeks, and pinch back leggy branches to encourage fullness.

COMMON NAME: TI PLANT, HAWAIIAN GOOD LUCK PLANT
BOTANICAL NAME: CORDYLINE FRUTICOSA
LIGHTING REQUIREMENTS: BRIGHT LIGHT
SOIL MOISTURE NEEDS: MODERATELY MOIST
PET FRIENDLY: NO

Ti Plant, also known as Hawaiian Good Luck Plant, is admired for its cane-like growth habit and long, lance-shaped foliage in shades of green, red, purple, pink or a combination of colors on one plant. It can grow up to three to six feet high indoors, depending on the variety and care. Ti Plant is often associated with good luck, protection, and prosperity in various cultures, particularly in Hawaii and Polynesia. Indoors, it grows best in stable humidity and bright, indirect light. Avoid direct sunlight, which can scorch the leaves. It is best to water with filtered or distilled water, as this plant can be sensitive to fluoride and chlorine. Use a well-draining potting mix with perlite or peat moss added to enhance drainage and moisture retention. Propagate by stem cuttings or offshoots in soil or water.

COMMON NAME: TI PLANT, HAWAIIAN GOOD LUCK PLANT
BOTANICAL NAME: CORDYLINE FRUTICOSA 'FLORIDA'
LIGHTING REQUIREMENTS: BRIGHT LIGHT
SOIL MOISTURE NEEDS: MODERATELY MOIST
PET FRIENDLY: NO

'Florida Red' is another variety of Ti Plant popular for its vibrant and bold coloration. The foliage is a striking mix of deep burgundy, red and pink hues, often intensifying in bright light. Like other Ti Plants, it typically reaches a height of three to six feet indoors and with maturity develops a woody cane-like stem, resembling a small tree. Cordyline fruticosa 'Florida' prefers stable humidity and bright, indirect light to maintain its color. Placement away from a western or southern window in a sunny room is ideal. Plant in a well-draining, rich potting soil containing perlite and peat moss and avoid watering with tap water, as the plant is sensitive to chlorine or fluoride, which can cause tip browning. Fertilize monthly during the growing season with a balanced fertilizer at half strength.

COMMON NAME: TRI-COLOR PRAYER PLANT
BOTANICAL NAME: STROMATHE SANGUINEA 'TRIOSTAR'
LIGHTING REQUIREMENTS: MEDIUM TO BRIGHT INDIRECT
SOIL MOISTURE NEEDS: MODERATELY MOIST
ADDITIONAL: PREFERS HIGH HUMIDITY
PET FRIENDLY: YES

A member of the Marantaceae family, and growing 2-3 feet tall by 1-2 feet wide, the variegated leaves of this beauty feature shades of pink, green, and white, with each leaf displaying a unique pattern. Like other prayer plants, they move their leaves in reflex to lighting and sometimes fold up at night, exposing burgundy-pink undersides. Locate Tri-Color Prayer Plant in a location with medium to bright indirect light and keep the top layer of soil moist, but not wet. Using distilled water is best and water weekly when the top layer of soil feels dry. Feed your plant with a well-balanced half strength fertilizer once a month during the growing season. Provide humidity by grouping with other plants, misting occasionally or use of a pebble tray.

COMMON NAME: UMBRELLA PLANT
BOTANICAL NAME: SCHEFFLERA ARBORICOLA
LIGHTING REQUIREMENTS: MEDIUM/DIFFUSED
SOIL MOISTURE NEEDS: MODERATELY MOIST
PET FRIENDLY: NO

The Umbrella Plant, Schefflera arboriciola, also known as Dwarf Umbrella Tree, is a popular houseplant for its attractive green or variegated foliage arranged in a circular pattern resembling an umbrella. Dwarf Umbrella Tree can grow to a height of three to six feet indoors but can be pruned to a smaller size, making it suitable for a variety of locations. It thrives in medium diffused light, but can tolerate lower light conditions, which will slow growth. Use a well-draining potting mix and water when the top two to three inches of the soil feels dry. Remove leggy growth to encourage fullness and feed monthly with a balanced fertilizer during the growing season. The larger variety of this plant is Schefflera actinophylla, which can reach 6-15 feet tall.

COMMON NAME: UMBRELLA PLANT
BOTANICAL NAME: SCHEFFLERA ARBORICOLA 'GOLD CAPELLA'
LIGHTING REQUIREMENTS: MEDIUM/DIFFUSED
SOIL MOISTURE NEEDS: MODERATELY MOIST
PET FRIENDLY: NO

'Gold Capella' is a striking cultivar of the Dwarf Umbrella Plant known for its vibrant, variegated foliage with bright green centers and golden-yellow variegation. It typically grows three to six feet indoors, depending on the size of the pot and pruning practices. To maintain its vibrant variegation, place in a location with medium diffused light and water when the top two to three inches of soil become dry. Avoid overwatering, as the plant is prone to root rot. Use a well-draining potting mix with added perlite or sand to improve drainage and feed monthly with a balanced fertilizer. Umbrella Plant thrives in moderate to high humidity but can adapt to average indoor conditions, making it an easy plant to care for. When grown in a smaller pot, S. arboricola can remain under two feet tall.

COMMON NAME: VARIEGATED SHELL GINGER
BOTANICAL NAME: ALPINIA ZERUMBET 'VARIEGATA'
LIGHTING REQUIREMENTS: MEDIUM TO BRIGHT/DIFFUSED
SOIL MOISTURE NEEDS: MODERATELY MOIST
ADDITIONAL: PREFERS HIGH HUMIDITY
PET FRIENDLY: YES

Displaying arching stems with long lance-shaped leaves striped with golden-yellow variegation, Variegated Shell Ginger makes a nice addition to a bright indoor location. This tropical plant can grow to three to four feet tall indoors, thrives in warmer temperatures between 65-80 degrees Fahrenheit (18-27 C) and prefers higher humidity, making it ideal for grouping with other plants. Use a well-draining potting mix meant for tropical plants and water when the top inch of soil feels dry. Keep the soil consistently moist, but never wet. Prune dead or yellowing leaves to maintain appearance and cut back overgrown stems in spring to encourage new growth. Feed monthly during spring and summer with a balanced liquid fertilizer.

COMMON NAME: VELVET CALATHEA
BOTANICAL NAME: CALATHEA RUFIBARBA
LIGHTING REQUIREMENTS: MEDIUM/DIFFUSED
SOIL MOISTURE NEEDS: MODERATELY MOIST
ADDITIONAL: PREFERS HIGH HUMIDITY
PET FRIENDLY: YES

The attraction of this plant is its soft, velvety medium green leaves that point upwards revealing deep burgundy undersides. Velvet Calathea grows to a height and width of 2-3 feet high by 1-2 feet wide at maturity and prefers a location with medium diffused lighting and a well-drained moderately moist soil, which should not be allowed to completely dry out. Calathea does not take well to tap water, so use distilled water or allow the water to sit out overnight before using. Placing a tray beneath the plant with pebbles and distilled water will help to provide the humidity the plant desires. Plant in an organically rich soil, and feed with a balanced fertilizer every four to six weeks during spring through fall to encourage new growth.

132

COMMON NAME: VENUS FLY TRAP
BOTANICAL NAME: DIONAEA MUSCIPULA
LIGHTING REQUIREMENTS: BRIGHT
SOIL MOISTURE NEEDS: HIGH
ADDITIONAL: PREFERS HIGH HUMIDITY
PET FRIENDLY: YES

Venus Fly Trap is a carnivorous plant with unique hinged, trap-like leaves lined with sensitive hairs that trap insects, making it a functional addition to your indoor collection. Growing to about five to six inches wide, provide this plant with at least twelve hours of bright, direct sunlight daily. Water with distilled or filtered water, keeping the soil consistently moist, but not wet and plant in a mix of sphagnum moss with sand or perlite. Since it prefers higher humidity, growing in a terrarium is ideal. If the plant does not catch insects naturally, feed it occasionally with live bugs such as ants or flies. One to two bugs a month is sufficient. This plant does go through a dormant state in late fall through winter.

COMMON NAME: WANDERING DUDE, SPIDERWORT, OR INCH PLANT
BOTANICAL NAME: TRADESCANTIA ZEBRINA
LIGHTING REQUIREMENTS: BRIGHT, INDIRECT
SOIL MOISTURE NEEDS: MODERATELY MOIST
PET FRIENDLY: NO

Tradescantia Zebrina is known for its attractive trailing foliage and tiny white or lavender blooms if conditions are right. It is best grown as a hanging plant, preferably near a western window in bright, indirect light while keeping the soil slightly moist. Avoid watering directly into the crown, as doing so may cause root rot. Regular fertilization at half strength during the growing season and misting foliage in winter keeps the plant at its best. Tradescantia tends to lose its leaves at the base as they mature, so it is important to pinch back about a fourth of the longer stems to encourage branching and fullness. Rooting cuttings is simple. Either bury the ends in potting soil and keep moist, or root directly in water and position in a sunny location.

COMMON NAME: WANDERING DUDE, SPIDERWORT
BOTANICAL NAME: TRANSDESCANTHA ALBIFLORA NAROUK
LIGHTING REQUIREMENTS: BRIGHT, INDIRECT
SOIL MOISTURE NEEDS: MODERATELY MOIST
PET FRIENDLY: NO

A newer cultivar of Tradescantia, 'Narouk' displays eye-catching striking, green, pink, and purple foliage. Thriving in bright, indirect light and a moderately moist soil, this species of Tradescantia has the same maintenance as 'Zebrina' but is a more compact plant with thicker stems and brighter color. It can be grown as a hanging plant, or on a desktop or windowsill where there is adequate light. As with other Tradescantia, fading color on foliage means the plant is not getting enough sun. To promote flowering , the plant should receive 6-8 hours of bright diffused light within three feet from a window. Water once a week when the top inch of soil is dry and mist or use a pebble tray in wintertime to prevent drying.

COMMON NAME: WAX PLANT
BOTANICAL NAME: HOYA 'OBOVATA SPLASH'
LIGHTING REQUIREMENTS: MEDIUM TO BRIGHT, INDIRECT
SOIL MOISTURE NEEDS: MODERATE
PET FRIENDLY: YES

Hoya is also called the Wax Plant due to its thick, wax-like leaves. It is the perfect choice for the beginner houseplant enthusiast and does well on a shelf or hanging basket, where it can cascade freely. Hoya is native to the tropical rainforests of eastern Asia and Australia where it grows as an epiphyte, as it gets its nutrients from the surrounding air and water. Plant Hoya in a rich peat-based soil, orchid mix or soil used for succulents or African Violet to ensure proper organic matter and drainage. Give this plant bright, indirect light, moderate watering, and allow the soil to dry out slightly in between waterings. Be sure to wet the soil thoroughly and allow excess moisture to drain into a saucer. This variety featured is unique compared to other Hoya in that it displays more robust leaves with silvery speckles or splashes, which are caused by tiny air pockets between the leaf tissue and cuticle. Increasing lighting and air circulation has been known to increase the "splash effect". To keep your Hoya looking its best, position it away from direct sunlight and feed with a well-balanced plant food at half strength once a month during the growing season. A mature Hoya will produce very fragrant porcelain-like flower clusters of pink blooms during the growing season when given the proper conditions.

If your Hoya is not yet blooming, it simply may not be ready yet, as it needs to be between three to seven years mature to do so. Do note that Hoya prefer to be somewhat root bound to produce flowers and withholding water for a few weeks in the springtime can encourage buds to form. The blooms form on the long vines or tendrils, so when pruning, always leave part of the stem for the flowers to form on.

COMMON NAME: WAX PLANT
BOTANICAL NAME: HOYA CARNOSA VARIEGATA
LIGHTING REQUIREMENTS: MEDIUM TO BRIGHT, INDIRECT
SOIL MOISTURE NEEDS: MODERATE
PET FRIENDLY: YES

Hoya carnosa Variegata displays beautiful, variegated foliage in shades of green and yellow with leaf margins highlighted with shades of creamy white and pink. At maturity and in ideal conditions, fragrant star-like blooms may develop with an aroma that is more intense at night. This species has the same needs as other Hoya, including medium to bright indirect light, moderate watering, and good drainage. Propagation is easy. Simply cut a long vine off the plant with at least two or more leaves at a few inches long and place the fresh cutting into water. Be sure only the top portion of the vine is in water, allowing to foliage to remain dry. Replace the water regularly to prevent disease and eventually the cutting will develop roots.

COMMON NAME: WAX PLANT, LUCKY HEART PLANT
BOTANICAL NAME: HOYA KERRII
LIGHTING REQUIREMENTS: MEDIUM TO BRIGHT, INDIRECT
SOIL MOISTURE NEEDS: MODERATE
PET FRIENDLY: YES

Known for its thick, heart-shaped leaves, which are often sold as single cuttings, Hoya 'Kerri' can grow as a vine with multiple leaves. Slow growing, it can trail or climb with support and may produce clusters of fragrant, star-shaped flowers at maturity. Plant in a well-draining potting mix and locate in medium to bright indirect light. It can tolerate some direct light, which will help with flowering, but avoid prolonged exposure to harsh afternoon sun. Allow the top one to two inches of soil to dry between waterings and avoid overwatering, which could lead to root rot. Hoya prefers to be slightly cramped in its pot and appreciates higher humidity but adapts to average household conditions. Occasional misting can suffice. Feed with a diluted balanced fertilizer during spring and summer.

COMMON NAME: WEEPING FIG
BOTANICAL NAME: FICUS BENJAMIN
LIGHTING REQUIREMENTS: BRIGHT
SOIL MOISTURE NEEDS: MODERATELY MOIST
PET FRIENDLY: NO

Featuring slender, arching branches with glossy, oval-shaped leaves, Weeping Fig can be grown as a small tree indoors, reaching between three and ten feet in height. Grow in bright, indirect light in a potting mix with good drainage and water when the top inch of soil is dry. Fertilize monthly during the growing season and prune to control size and shape. Pruning is best done in late winter to early spring when sap production is low. Avoid sudden changes, as this plant can be sensitive. Avoid overwatering, underwatering, or changing location, as these can cause leaves to drop.

COMMON NAME: ZEBRA PLANT, ZEBRA HAWORTHIA
BOTANICAL NAME: HAWORTHIA FASCIATA 'BIG BAND'
LIGHTING REQUIREMENTS: BRIGHT INDIRECT LIGHT
SOIL MOISTURE NEEDS: LOW
PET FRIENDLY: YES

The Zebra Plant is a succulent admired for its pointed, fleshy green leaves with white horizontal striped foliage, giving it a zebra-like appearance. Having a compact nature and growing to just four to eight inches tall and wide, it is an excellent low maintenance houseplant for small spaces. Plant in a well-draining cactus or succulent mix and keep in bright, indirect light. Avoid the harsh afternoon sun, as it can scorch the tips of the leaves. Allow the soil to dry completely between waterings and water sparingly in winter. Soft or mushy leaves indicate overwatering. Remove any dried or damaged leaves to maintain health and feed the plant with a diluted fertilizer once a month during the growing season. Small, tubular white flowers on long stems may appear in late spring or summer.

COMMON NAME: ZZ PLANT
BOTANICAL NAME: ZAMIOCULCAS ZAMIIFOLIA
LIGHTING REQUIREMENTS: BRIGHT INDIRECT, TOLERANT OF LOW LIGHT
SOIL MOISTURE NEEDS: LOW
PET FRIENDLY: NO, MILDLY TOXIC

A low maintenance houseplant, ZZ Plant is slow growing, reaching a mature size of two to three feet indoors. Displaying glossy, dark green, waxy leaves in a feather-like arrangement on thick, upright stems, makes for an attractive addition. Plant in a well-draining potting soil and locate in bright, indirect light. Thick rhizomes store water, decreasing water needs, making it drought tolerant. Water only when the soil is allowed to dry. A sign of overwatering is indicated by yellowing leaves. ZZ Plant is not a heavy feeder. Fertilize with a balanced plant food every two to three months during the growing season. Avoid contact with the sap, as it can cause irritation to the skin or eyes. With minimal care, this selection is excellent for both the beginner and experienced plant enthusiast.

Chapter 2: Flowering Plants

Flowering houseplants bring a touch of the rainforest to your home, with the presence of colorful and sometimes fragrant blooms. Imagine enhancing your indoor surroundings with the beautiful and abundant blooms of African Violet, Phalaenopsis Orchid, or Kalanchoe or seize the opportunity of experiencing the more unexpected blooms of a Jade Plant, ZZ Plant, Snake Plant or Hoya when the conditions are right. Most flowering houseplants are monoecious, meaning they possess both female and male structures which allows them to self-pollinate. Depending on your houseplant, the blooms produced can be true flowers, or structures known as bracts. In botany, bracts are modified or specialized leaves with the appearance of flower petals that in nature protect the reproductive parts of the plant from extreme environmental conditions or insects. In many cases the colorful bracts play the role of attracting beneficial pollinators to the plant. Common houseplants displaying bracts include Poinsettia, Peace Lily, Chinese Evergreen, Anthurium, and Bromeliad. Next time you look at a Poinsettia, behold the colorful leaves supplying interest for months are bracts surrounding the central clusters of greenish-yellow flowers.

Besides adding interest many flowering houseplants are known to purify the air and improve overall well-being, while creating improved mood, increased productivity by reducing stress, and boosting overall happiness. Their diverse variety of colors and shapes of blooms serve as focal points while creating a visually appealing and healthy surrounding in your home.

AFRICAN VIOLET

AMARYLLIS

ANTHURIUM

BEGONIA

BIRD OF PARADISE

BROMELIAD

CLIVIA

CYCLAMEN

KALANCHOE

PEACE LILY

PHALANGES ORCHID

POINSETTIA

SPRING CACTUS	THANKSGIVING CACTUS
CHRISTMAS CACTUS	MEZZO PLANT
LIVING STONE	PURPLE HEART

 Chapter 3: Trailing & Climbing Plants

Do you have limited space, are you looking to elevate plants away from children and pets or simply looking for decorating ideas? Trailing and climbing plants are excellent candidates for displaying from ceilings or walls while utilizing vertical space. This makes them ideal for smaller living areas or rooms with limited floor space and allows you to enjoy the beauty of greenery while experimenting with different plant varieties, pot styles, and hanging techniques. Many indoor plants such as pothos, spider plants, Tradescantia, and philodendrons, are suitable for hanging or staking, and valued for their resilience and low maintenance requirements, making them perfect for busy individuals or those new to plant care. Trailing and climbing plants complement various interior design styles, from modern and minimalist to bohemian and tropical, enhancing the overall aesthetic appeal of your home.

Another advantage is that these plants also can help regulate indoor climate by providing shade and moisture, especially in areas exposed to direct sunlight or dry air. Some plants can even absorb sound waves, making them natural sound dampeners. Hanging plants strategically placed in areas with high noise levels, such as near busy streets or in open-plan living spaces, can help reduce noise pollution. Whether you are a seasoned plant enthusiast or just beginning to explore the world of indoor gardening, incorporating hanging plants can be a rewarding and enjoyable experience.

BOSTON FERN

ENGLISH IVY

FISHBONE CACTUS

HOYA

HOYA VARIEGATED

PINK LADY

POTHOS	PURPLE HEART

SPIDER PLANT	SPIDERWORT

SPIDERWORT/INCH PLANT	STRING OF PEARLS

STRING OF TEARS

STRING OF WATERMELONS

VARIEGATED POTHOS

MEZZO PLANT

MONSTERA

SWISS CHEESE PLANT

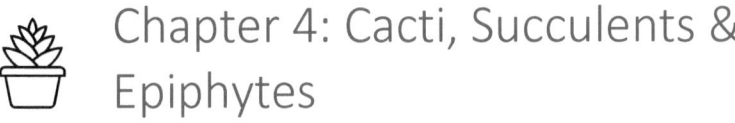 Chapter 4: Cacti, Succulents & Epiphytes

Among the various types of houseplants, succulents, cacti, and epiphytes stand out for their unique characteristics and ease of care which makes these plants popular choices for indoor gardening enthusiasts. Succulents and Cacti are renowned for their ability to store water in their fleshy leaves, stems, or roots, making them resilient to dry conditions. They are relatively low-maintenance plants requiring bright light, well-draining soil, minimal fertilization, and only occasional watering.

Epiphytes like Tillandsias and Orchids simply use their hosts for support. They thrive in minimal soil or even without soil and derive moisture and nutrients from the air making them versatile options for vertical gardens, terrariums, and unique hanging displays. Epiphytes often have stunning foliage and flowers, adding a touch of exotic beauty to your indoor space. With proper care, including regular misting or soaking and adequate air circulation, these plants can flourish and become captivating focal points in your home. Another attribute is that certain species of succulents and epiphytes such as Aloe, Snake Plant, Tillandsias and Orchids improve indoor environment by removing harmful toxins from the air.

Incorporating succulents, cacti, and epiphytes into your indoor garden offers many benefits including greenery, air purification and low maintenance. These resilient and captivating plants are sure to thrive and bring joy to your living space.

AIR PLANT	ALOE (MEDICINAL)
ALOE (SPIRAL)	ALOE (FAN)
CACTUS	MISTLETOE CACTUS

BROMELIAD

LACE ALOE

ET'S FINGERS JADE

LIVING STONE

MEXICAN ROSETTE

SNAKE PLANT

CHRISTMAS CACTUS	SPRING CACTUS
THANKSGIVING CACTUS	MEZZO PLANT
JADE PLANT	ZEBRA PLANT

# Chapter 5: Low Maintenance Plants

If you are looking to add some greenery to your home without the hassle, low maintenance houseplants are the perfect solution. These plants are resilient, requiring minimal care and attention while still providing all the benefits of indoor greenery. Examples of low maintenance houseplants include but are not limited to Snake Plant (Sansevieria), ZZ Plant (Zamioculcas Zamiifolia), Spider Plant (Chlorophytum comosum), Peace Lily (Spathiphyllum), Pothos (Epipremnum aureum), Cast Iron Plant (Aspidistra elatior) and Aloe Vera. Known for its resilience and air-purifying qualities, Snake Plant thrives in low light conditions and requires minimal watering, while ZZ Plant is virtually indestructible, tolerating low light, infrequent watering, and neglect. Its glossy, dark green leaves add a touch of elegance to any room. Spider Plant are hardy and adaptable, making them ideal for forgetful gardeners. They produce offshoots that can be easily propagated into new plants, adding to their charm. Peace Lily is a favorite among low maintenance plant enthusiasts. It thrives in low light and only requires occasional watering, while Pothos is known for its trailing vines and easy-care nature. It can tolerate a variety of light conditions, from low to bright indirect light, and only needs watering when the soil is dry. Cast Iron Plant is true to its name, incredibly tough and can survive in low light, fluctuating temperatures, and drought-like conditions. It is an excellent choice for beginners or those with challenging environments. Apart from its medicinal properties, Aloe Vera is a low maintenance succulent that adds a touch of green to your space. It prefers bright, indirect light and infrequent watering, making it suitable for busy individuals. Other low maintenance houseplants include Parlor Palm (Chamaedorea Elegans), Lucky Bamboo (Dracaena sanderiana) and Zebra Plant (Haworthia fasciata) among others. Like Aloe, Zebra Plant prefers bright light from a southern or western window while Parlor Palm and Lucky Bamboo will tolerate lower light conditions.

Care Tips for Low Maintenance Houseplants: Most low maintenance plants thrive in indirect light, although some can tolerate low light conditions. Place them near windows or areas with filtered sunlight for optimal growth. Water them only when the top inch of soil feels dry to the touch and avoid overwatering your plants, as this can lead to root rot. As a proactive measure, use pots with drainage holes to prevent waterlogging. Low maintenance plants generally require minimal fertilization. Use a balanced liquid fertilizer diluted to half-strength during the growing season (spring and summer) to support healthy growth. Trim yellowing or dead leaves and remove faded blooms to promote new growth and maintain the plant's appearance. Check for pests regularly and address any issues promptly to prevent infestations.

By choosing low maintenance houseplants and following simple care guidelines, you can enjoy the benefits of indoor greenery without the stress of intensive plant care. These plants are sure to thrive in your home environment, bringing nature's beauty indoors effortlessly.

ALOE

CAST IRON PLANT

LUCKY BAMBOO

PEACE LILY

PARLOR PALM

POTHOS

SNAKE PLANT

SPIDER PLANT

ZEBRA PLANT

ZZ PLANT

BROMELIAD

CACTI

# Chapter 6: Air Purifying Plants

The first studies examining the ability of plants to purify the air started back in the late 1980's when NASA conducted the Clean Air Study, a group of experiments investigating the possible role of plants to improve air quality in space stations. Certain houseplants including African Violet, Spider Plant, Pothos and Snake Plant have been found to possess the ability to remove toxic chemicals from indoor environments through a process known as phytoremediation, in which the plant absorbs harmful compounds through microscopic pores, or stomata in their leaves, thus reducing the concentration of VOCs (volatile organic chemicals) like benzene, formaldehyde, and trichloroethylene. These toxins enter a living environment with everyday cleaning materials, paints, varnishes, carpeting, and manufactured furniture or enter from outdoor vehicles, nearby industry, or pesticides. Along with removing these volatile organic chemicals from the air, plants absorb carbon dioxide and emit oxygen through photosynthesis. More recently, the Famulari Theory addresses that certain plants can better reduce the transmission of airborne viruses based on their leaf structure, presence of stomata, trichomes, dense leaf growth, and higher transpiration rate. Various greening practices can be applied to sites such as train stations, restaurants, workspaces, and home offices to reduce the infectiousness of the airborne flu virus, in return reducing the occurrence of respiratory issues such as allergies and colds; therefore, leading to a healthier environment.

AFRICAN VIOLET	**AIR PLANT**

ALOE VERA	**CHINESE EVERGREEN**

CROTON	**SONG OF JAMAICA**

FIDDLE LEAF FIG

FISHBONE CACTUS

GOLDEN POTHOS

MOTH ORCHID

NEVER-NEVER PLANT

ARALIA FABIAN

CAT PALM

DIEFFENBACHIA

PEPEROMIA

DRACAENA

PRAYER PLANT

PRAYER PLANT (FISHBONE)

RATTLESNAKE PLANT

RUBBER TREE

SNAKE PLANT

SPIDER PLANT

CALATHEA FASCIATA

BOSTON FERN

DRAGON TREE	ARECA PALM
LADY PALM	PARLOR PALM
PONYTAIL PALM	ENGLISH IVY

Chapter 7: Pet Friendly Plants

Pets and plants can coexist but not all plants are pet friendly and not all pets are plant friendly. If you are like me and possess a love for both pets and houseplants, you can successfully obtain this relationship. First, let us define what is meant by toxic verses pet friendly. Some plants which are considered toxic contain harmful compounds such as calcium oxalates, which are found in the form of tiny crystals. These crystals cause irritation and discomfort when they meet with the skin, mouth, or digestive tract, and can cause mild to severe oral irritation, swelling and gastrointestinal upset. Some common houseplants to avoid include Dieffenbachia, Philodendron, Snake Plant, Rubber Plant, Jade and ZZ Plant, Peace Lily, and Sago Palm. The good news is that there are several houseplants considered to be pet friendly, as no part of the plant is toxic. Some pet-friendly houseplants include but are not limited to Parlor Palm, Spider Plant, Boston Fern, Areca Palm, African Violet, Prayer Plant, Calathea, Moth Orchid, and Air Plants.

Here are some tips. When purchasing concentrate on those to be pet-friendly and supervise your pet when you bring the plants home, as they could spark some interest. Place plants out of reach by elevating them on a stand, shelf, or displaying them as a hanging basket. Also, teach your pet not to dig or chew on plants through positive reinforcement and reward for good behavior. The relationship between your green and furry friends can be achieved by simply taking a few steps to create an atmosphere of well-being and beauty in your living space.

AFRICAN VIOLET

AIR PLANT

EASTER (SPRING) CACTUS

FRIENDSHIP PLANT

FISHBONE PRAYER PLANT

MEXICAN SNOWBALL

MOTH ORCHID

NERVE PLANT

NEVER-NEVER PLANT

PEPEROMIA

PALM (ARECA, BAMBOO)

PALM (CAT PALM)

PARLOR PALM

PEACOCK PLANT

PONYTAIL PALM

PRAYER PLANT

RATTLESNAKE PLANT

SPIDER PLANT

THANKSGIVING CACTUS

CHRISTMAS CACTUS

TRI-COLOR PRAYER PLANT

VELVET CALATHEA

CALATHEA FASCIATA

CALATHEA WHITESTAR

Chapter 8: Growing Herbs Indoors

Growing herbs indoors is a wonderful way to add fresh flavors to your meals, brighten your living space and bring a bit of nature to your home. Even if you have limited space, you can create a thriving herb garden on a windowsill or kitchen counter. Most herbs need warm temperatures between 65-75 degrees F (18-24 C) and plenty of sunlight to thrive, ideally 6-8 hours per day. Place your herb garden near a sunny, south-facing window or consider using a grow light, especially during the winter months. LED lights can provide an energy-efficient solution. Plant in a well-draining potting mix designed for herbs or make use of a hydroponic system and feed sparingly. An organic plant food at half strength every 6-8 weeks is best. Water regularly, keeping the soil moist, but not wet. When choosing herbs for growing indoors, it is important to select varieties that adapt well to indoor environments. Here are some top choices.

Basil: Basil is fast-growing and easily grown from seed directly in pots indoors. Varieties such as Greek Basil and Spicy Globe Basil are naturally compact and grow well in smaller spaces. Basil prefers a moderately moist soil and warmer temperatures between 70-80 degrees F (21-27 C). Avoid placing it near cold drafts and pinch off tops to encourage bushier growth.

Rosemary: This woody herb has fragrant needle-like leaves that add flavor to a variety of dishes. It prefers well-drained soil and bright sunlight and does best near a south-facing window. Recommended varieties for indoor growth include Blue Boy, Tuscan Blue and Spice Islands, which tend to stay smaller.

Thyme: Thyme has small, flavorful leaves that are excellent for soups, stews, and roasted meats. English Thyme, Lemon Thyme and Creeping Thyme are well suited for containers, require six hours of bright light, temperatures between 60-75 degrees F (16-24 C) and low humidity.

Parsley: Flat-leaf and Curly Parsley both grow well indoors, though flat parsley has a more robust flavor. To keep the plant productive, avoid cutting more than one-third of the plant at a time. Parsley seeds can germinate slowly. To speed up germination, soak seeds in warm water for a few hours before planting or purchase as young plants.

Mint: Peppermint and Spearmint are popular indoor choices and best grown in bright, indirect light for at least 4-6 hours per day. Since it grows rapidly, an 8–10-inch pot is best. Position near a sunny east or west facing window where it can receive morning or late afternoon light. Mint thrives in soil rich in organic matter.

Oregano: Start Oregano from seeds, cuttings or a developed plant and grow in 6-8 hours of sunlight. This hardy herb grows well in a sandy, well-draining cactus or succulent soil or mix perlite to regular potting soil to improve drainage.

Cilantro: Cilantro grows best in cool conditions between 50-75 degrees F (10-24 C) and requires a sunny spot to survive. Gently crush the seeds to split them in half and soak in water for 24 hours before planting.

Chives: Chives bring a mild onion-like flavor to dishes and are ideal for indoor gardens. They require 5-8 hours of direct sunlight per day and a well-draining moist soil.

Chapter 9: Maintenance Tips

Insects & Pests: Houseplant pests can become a nuisance, but if monitored regularly, can easily be prevented, and controlled. To help prevent pests, try to avoid rapid changes in environment around your plants. Do not allow plant leaves to become exposed to cold drafts, such as touching window glass and avoid sudden movement to different lighting conditions. Also, avoid over-fertilizing, as an increased amount of nitrogen in leaves can attract insects who feed on the plant for nutrients. If you do suspect insect damage, spray the plant with an insecticidal soap to remedy it. A more natural approach is to remove all visible insects with an alcohol swab. Then spray with a homemade mixture of one cup of rubbing alcohol with a few drops of dish soap dissolved in a quart of water. Another method proven successful is to rub down both sides of the leaves with a soft cloth saturated with warm soapy dish detergent. Repeat whichever method you choose once or twice a week until the insects are no longer visible. Some of the most common pests affecting houseplants include mealybug, spider mite, aphids, scale, thrips, and fungus gnats.

Mealybug: Mealybug are soft-bodied insects that are covered with a white, waxy cottony material that protects them from heat and humidity. The plants most affected by mealybugs are soft-stemmed and succulent plants including Jade, Hoya, Cactus, Croton and African Violet..

Spider Mite: Spider mites appear as tiny white or yellow spots on the leaves. If you look closely you will see streaks or stripes and small delicate webs on the corners of stems and beneath the plants foliage. Plants prone to spider mite include Fiddle Leaf Fig, English Ivy, Spider Plant, Pothos and Dracaena.

Aphids: Aphids are tiny pear-shaped sucking insects, usually light green in color, that are attracted to the soft growing parts of a plant that are high in nitrogen. Signs of aphid damage include curling, yellow leaves and stunted plant growth.

Scale: Scale appears as small brown oval shaped bumps on the surface or undersides of foliage or on stems. Once they feed on the plant, they leave a sticky honeydew substance which becomes more noticable as the population increases.

FIGURE 1: MEALYBUGS

FIGURE 2: SPIDER MITE

FIGURE 3: APHIDS

FIGURE 4: SCALE

Thrips: Thrips are tiny insects which can be difficult to see with the naked eye and appear as small dark or yellowish spots on the undersides of leaves. These insects feed on plant cells by puncturing the tissue and sucking out the contents, causing discolored silvery patches or brown spots on foliage. These pests can effectively be controlled by isolating the plant, removing heavily infested leaves, and spraying with an insecticide or neem oil. Since thrips can be challenging to eradicate, several treatments may be necessary. Plants most affected by thrips include monstera, pothos and philodendron. Here is an example of thrips and damage left on the undersides of leaves on philodendron.

FIGURE 5: THRIPS   FIGURE 6: THRIP DAMAGE

Fungus Gnats: Fungus gnats are small mosquito-like insects that lie in the top two to three inches of growing medium and feed on decaying plant matter. They are relatively harmless but can become problematic to roots if the population becomes too large. To control these insects, allow plants to dry out in between waterings, which will decrease their survival. There are other methods of deterring them, including adding a layer of sand or fine gravel to the surface of the soil to shy them away from laying eggs. If the population is more severe, the best control is to apply a product containing BTI, or Bacillus thuringiensis israelensis, an EPA approved soil bacterium used to control larvae of these pests. Additionally, the use of sticky tapes can be used to catch the adults.

Yellowing or Browning Leaves: Yellowing or browning leaves can be a sign of various issues, such as overwatering, underwatering, nutrient deficiency or possible pests. The most common error encountered is overwatering. Yellowing mushy foliage is associated with too much watering while browning crispy foliage indicates too little watering or lack of humidity. Feel down into the soil to check for moisture. Especially if the leaves are turning yellow or emerging already yellow in color, gently lift the plant from its pot and inspect the roots. Healthy plant roots are firm and lighter in color, while dark mushy roots indicate a condition known as root rot. Repot the plant in fresh potting mix, adjust watering practices, and make sure there is proper drainage. In addition to yellowing, stunted growth or leaf drop can be a sign of nitrogen deficiency. Remember, it is better to water deeper and less often, while allowing any excess water to drain from the plant.

Additional Care: Once your houseplants are established in the correct growing conditions, a little tender loving care goes a long way in keeping them healthy. Practice simple routines including removing dust from foliage, pruning, removing damaged or dying leaves, and repotting when needed. Since plants breathe through their leaves, it is beneficial to mist their foliage with a spray bottle, wipe with a damp clean cloth or paper

towel or place the entire plant in the sink or shower and clean with a gentle spray.

Alternate Lighting: If your natural lighting is insufficient, another option is artificial lighting. Generally, plants need blue wavelength light for foliage development and red wavelength light for flowering and fruiting. There are different types of artificial lighting to choose from including fluorescent and incandescent, LED, or HID indoor grow lights. Fluorescent grow lights are the most popular and economical choice for supplementing low to medium light during wintertime or for starting seeds and can be placed closer to the plant. Since some generic bulbs are higher in blue wavelengths, look for one with full spectrum lighting and place it about a foot away from your houseplant. Incandescent lighting gives off more red (longer wavelengths) and are excellent for low light houseplants but give off a lot of heat. They should be positioned at least 18-24 inches away from the plant to avoid scorching and can be used along with florescent lighting. Monitor and adjust the distance until you have the ideal lighting. Next are LED and HID artificial lighting, both more costly but exceptionally energy efficient, longer lasting and providing an ideal spectrum range, hence the efficiency can outweigh the cost. Whichever mode of artificial lighting you choose, be sure to purchase bulbs that produce both blue and red wavelengths.

Propagation: There are several methods of propagating houseplants. These include cuttings, division, offsets, layering, and seeds. **Cuttings**: Taking cuttings is one of the easiest and most common practices for rooting many species of indoor plants including Tradescantia, Pothos, Jade Plant, and Ivy, just to name a few. It is performed by taking a healthy cutting, ensuring that it has a node where leaves and roots form, and placed into a medium such as water or potting mix to allow roots to develop. Cut at a forty-five-degree angle just below the node and be sure to remove any extra leaves so that they are not exposed to the water or soil. When grown in soil, cuttings can be dipped into a rooting hormone, placed into fresh potting soil, and kept moist for optimum results. When rooting in water, be sure to change the water regularly to prevent bacterial growth. Place the cuttings in a location with bright, indirect light. Avoid direct sunlight, as it can be too intense for young plants. **Division**: Division involves splitting a mature plant into smaller sections with roots. This works well with plants having multiple stems or bulbs, such as Philodendron, Peace Lily, Snake Plant, ZZ Plant and Cat Palm. The best time to divide most houseplants is during their active growing season, typically in spring or early summer. It is recommended to water a day or two before dividing the plant to facilitate its removal. Be sure to use a clean, sharp spade or pruning shears to form clean cuts to minimize damage, while getting a good balance of roots and foliage. If the plant is root-bound, gently loosen the roots with your fingers before replanting. Relocate each new section into a fresh potting mix and keep the soil moist, but not wet. Avoid any fertilizing for a few weeks until your plant becomes established in its new home. **Offsets**: Some plants such as Spider Plant, Aloe, Bromeliad and Haworthia produce offsets, or baby plants from stems or around the base. Wait until these baby plants are large enough to have their own root system and then gently remove them from the mother plant. The new plantings should be located at a depth where the roots are just covered, in a location with the proper lighting conditions for the plant and with the soil kept moist. **Layering**: Layering can occur when a stem produces roots while still attached to the parent plant. The new plants can be separated and replanted once the roots develop. **Seeds**: This method can be used for seed producing flowering houseplants such as African Violet and Begonia but does require time and patience.

Pruning: Some houseplants such as Tradescantia Zebrina are prone to losing foliage near the top as they push out new growth at the bottom, which is all part of the natural life cycle. To keep your plant viable, maintain a regular practice of pinching off the longer shoots about a quarter of the way to promote fullness and to drive the plant's energy back up into the crown. Other houseplants such as Bonsai Ficus, Rubber Plant, Pothos, English Ivy, String of Pearls, Spider Plant, Jade, Thanksgiving-Christmas, or Spring Cactus also benefit from pinching off longer stems to promote fullness. It is also common for some varieties of houseplants to naturally shed their older or lower leaves from their crown as part of their growth process. These plants include, but are not limited to Dragon Tree, Yucca and Ponytail Palm.

How do I Get My Houseplants to Bloom?: I am asked this question all the time, especially when it comes to succulents, such as Thanksgiving Cactus. Some houseplants need a change in lighting and temperature to trigger blooms. In the case of Thanksgiving Cactus, I have mine on a southwestern facing windowsill in a room with skylights. The plants sense the change in lighting and the cooler nighttime temperatures during fall and winter, hence triggering the plant to produce buds and blooms from early November all the way through January. I feed mine with a balanced houseplant fertilizer at half strength from June through August and remove faded blooms to encourage even more buds and blooms during flowering time. This same technique can also be used to promote blooms on Christmas or Spring Cactus, Jade Plant and Echeveria!

Some houseplants, such as African Violet, do not require a dormant period, which allows them to bloom all year, but they do prefer a more confined space, and other factors such as improper lighting, cold drafts or extreme temperatures can also inhibit flowering. If your African Violets are not producing blooms, first try improving the lighting. The best location is an eastern or northern exposure with diffused light or within two to three feet of a northwestern window. Too little light will prevent blooming, while too much direct sunlight can scorch the leaves. Another tip is to groom off any faded leaves and flowers and apply a low nitrogen, high phosphorus plant food every four to six weeks, which will help to promote blooms. If the plant is in a pot which has a lot of extra space, you may consider repotting it for best results. An additional tip is that I have the most successful blooms with my African Violets that are in self-watering pots. It seems to supply just the right amount of moisture and humidity to keep the plant at its best.

Another plant I often get questioned about is Peace Lily. Peace Lily start to produce blooms in early spring as daylight hours increase. Like African Violet, they prefer a smaller sized pot, but not to be root bound, and a location with diffused lighting, such as a northern or eastern exposure with feeding during the active growing season. If watering, lighting, and fertilization remains the same, the most common reason Peace Lily stop flowering is either the plant has been exposed to excessive heat or cold draft, which will inhibit its growth or the pot is too small, and the plant has become rootbound. Yellowing or browning leaves near the base of the plant or stunted growth are signs of being root bound, and the remedy is to relocate the plant into a slightly larger home.

Trouble Shooting: Certain plants such as Fiddle Leaf Fig or Weeping Fig can be "fickle" when it comes to getting them adjusted. Your tree will be sensitive to temperature changes and does not like to be moved. It may drop a couple of leaves in the transition from greenhouse to your home, but that is normal. Within a couple of weeks your tree should stabilize. If your plant continues to shed leaves it may be a sign of not enough light. If the leaves become dry or brittle where the rim of the leaves start to brown and curl in, or if small reddish-brown spots appear on the bottom on the leaves that show through, it is a sign of inconsistency or underwatering. If your tree's leaves start to brown and fall off because the soil is moist, allow the plant to dry out slightly, then resume watering while monitoring how the plant reacts. Misting daily or the use of a pebble tray can also help to provide moisture to the plant.

If you want to maintain a fuller plant, the best time to prune your Fiddle Leaf or Weeping Fig is during spring or summer when it is pushing out new growth. Find the top of the main stem and prune just above the node where the leaves and stem meet and gently dab the area to remove extra sap. Wear gloves as the sap is mildly toxic and can irritate your skin.

Basically, if a plant is stressed by lack of sunlight, too much or too little watering, or lack of fertilization, it is advisable to evaluate each factor and improve the overall environment of your green friend. A little tender loving care can go a long way.

Some Interesting Plant Facts: The red undersides of leaves on some tropical plants such as Calathea and Maranta is caused by a pigment called **anthocyanin**, which primarily functions as a form of photoprotection, preventing damage from too much sunlight. The pigment also acts to absorb excess light that might otherwise be lost, allowing the capturing of more light for photosynthesis. You will notice the red undersides are more exposed when the leaves fold upwards at night. This evolutionary adaption has developed in tropical plants that live in the lower levels of the rainforest where light is limited. If the lighting in your growing habitat is adequate, the plant may not have the need to produce as much as the anthocyanin pigment. Another

184

phenomenon that can occur is known as guttation. You may notice visible water droplets on the leaves or dripping down, especially from your larger-leaved tropical planta such as Monstera and Philodendron, usually occurring in the early morning or late evening when temperatures are cooler, and humidity is high. **Guttation** is a perfectly normal and natural process in which a houseplant releases excess water through specialized pores on their leaves called hydathodes, often occurring when humidity is high, and the plant has absorbed more water that it can transpire.

In conclusion, the world of indoor gardening extends far beyond just pure aesthetics. A vital connection with nature, our green companions bring well-being, air quality, and overall joy to our living spaces. When bringing your houseplants home, nurture them and reflect on the role they play in fostering a healthier, more balanced environment for both us and the planet.

Acknowledgements

In the world of gardening and writing, so much is learned from colleagues and conversations with others who share a passion of all things green. I am grateful for the kindness and helpfulness of two local nurseries here on Long Island, Fantastic Gardens and Bayport Flower Houses. They graciously welcomed me to spend hours at a time photographing their huge collection of houseplants, while workers shared their vast knowledge and expertise. I would also like to thank Stevie Famulari, Gds, who I had the pleasure of meeting and working with. Stevie is a green design specialist, professor, author, and founder of Engaging Green. Her Famulari Theory explains how certain houseplants can reduce the infectiousness of airborne flu viruses throughout workplaces, restaurants, hospitals, transportation and living spaces, thus creating a healthier environment wherever people gather. Stevie has broadened my appreciation and knowledge of indoor plants even more than I could have possibly imagined.

About the Author

Involved in the horticultural industry for over 28 years Lee Miller spends her days designing gardens for others and working with plants on a constant basis. Along with her gardening career, and appreciation for all things green, she proudly tends to an extensive collection of indoor plants, which she has enjoyed for more than 40 years. Known in the gardening world, Lee Miller has been involved as a contributing writer for various magazine publications and has participated as a presenter for local universities, various gardening clubs and horticultural conferences. To keep current in the field, she is an active member of several garden related organizations, constantly learning and sharing her knowledge with others. Lee Miller is also the author of five previous publications, including *A Guide to Northeastern Gardening, Landscape Design Combinations, Dream, Garden, Grow!-Musings of a Lifetime Gardener, Gardening by Month: A Monthly Guide to Planning the Northeastern & Mid-Atlantic Garden* and *Shade Gardening for the Northeast and Mid-Atlantic*, each sharing her experiences and knowledge as a seasoned gardener. With trowel in hand since the age of five, her passion for both outdoor and indoor gardening continues to grow.

Index

www.ingramcontent.com/pod-product-compliance
Lightning Source LLC
Chambersburg PA
CBHW040854120626
46551CB00001B/11